GRAND PRIX WINNERS

WINNERS

MOTOR RACING HEROES SINCE 1950

GRAND PRIX WINNERS

MOTOR RACING HEROES SINCE 1950

Denis Jenkinson

Nigel Roebuck

Alan Henry

Maurice Hamilton

Steve Small

GOOD YEAR / #1 in Racing

HAZLETON PUBLISHING LTD, RICHMOND, SURREY

Publisher
RICHARD POULTER

Business Development Manager
SIMON MAURICE

Production Manager
GEORGE GREENFIELD

Art Editor
STEVE SMALL

Managing Editor
PETER LOVERING

Publishing Assistant
CLARE RAGGETT

Pictured on the front cover are:

Top row, left to right:
Juan Manuel Fangio*
Jim Clark
Ayrton Senna
Alain Prost
Jack Brabham*
Photos: Goddard Picture Library and LAT*

Middle:
Damon Hill, at the wheel of his
Williams FW17-Renault
Photo: Mike Hewitt / Allsport

Bottom row, left to right:
Michael Schumacher
Emerson Fittipaldi
Damon Hill*
Nigel Mansell
Niki Lauda
*Photos: LAT and Nigel Snowdon**

Title page
Michael Schumacher, Damon Hill and
Jean Alesi share the podium after the
1994 British Grand Prix at Silverstone.
Photo: LAT

Right:
Nigel Mansell was denied the World
Championship in 1986 but made
amends six years later.
Photo: Nigel Snowdon

Top right:
Nelson Piquet celebrates his first Grand
Prix win with Emerson Fittipaldi and
Riccardo Patrese, Long Beach 1980.
Photo: Nigel Snowdon

Back cover, main photo:
Ferrari's Gerhard Berger has nine
Grand Prix wins to his credit.
Photo: Nigel Snowdon

Back cover, bottom photo:
Mario Andretti, World Champion for
Lotus in 1978.

This second edition published in 1995
by Hazleton Publishing Limited,
3 Richmond Hill, Richmond, Surrey TW10 6RE.

ISBN: 1-874557-66-7

Printed in Great Britain by Butler and Tanner Limited,
Frome, Somerset.

DISTRIBUTORS
United Kingdom
Bookpoint Ltd, 39 Milton Park
Abingdon, Oxfordshire OX14 4TD

North America
Motorbooks International, PO Box 1
729 Prospect Ave.
Osecola, Wisconsin 54020, USA

Australia
Technical Book and Magazine Co. Pty
289-299 Swanston Street, Melbourne
Victoria 3000

New Zealand
David Bateman Ltd, 'Golden Heights'
32-34 View Road
Glenfield, Auckland 10

South Africa
Motorbooks, 341 Jan Smuts Avenue
Craighall Park, Johannesburg

INTRODUCTION

G RAND PRIX drivers, it has often been said, are a breed apart. Even the least successful of them possesses an extraordinary cocktail of contrasting qualities – instant reactions, boundless competitiveness, fingertip delicacy, raw courage – that most of us can only wonder at. The casual spectator has only to watch a modern F1 car storming through a fast corner with scarcely a lift of the throttle to be reminded of that. However, even within this small group of exceptional individuals there is another, exclusive élite: the Grand Prix *winners*. In any era there are only a handful of men who are blessed with the exceptional gifts, iron will and, perhaps, good fortune to push on to the summit of motor racing's highest peak when others have been forced to abandon their attempt down on the lower slopes.

This book profiles every driver to win a World Championship Grand Prix outright since the introduction of the World Championship for Drivers in 1950. However, it is more than a simple catalogue of their achievements. Bringing together the talents of a number of outstanding motor sport writers and photographers, we have attempted to capture the essence of the men who have tasted victory at the highest level of the sport.

Denis Jenkinson, Nigel Roebuck, Alan Henry, Maurice Hamilton and Steve Small have each concentrated on a decade of Grand Prix racing, spotlighting the Grand Prix winners in those eras. To avoid repetition, drivers have generally been included in the decade during which they were most successful, with the exception of those whose triumphs have been spread throughout particularly lengthy careers.

We have not forgotten those who, while they failed to reach the summit, nevertheless came within sight of it: those drivers who enjoyed distinguished careers and were perhaps unfortunate not to have been rewarded with that elusive Grand Prix victory. They are featured at the end of each section.

In addition, we have included two colour sections illustrating many of the leading World Championship contenders in their true element – in action at the wheel of a Grand Prix car.

Last, but certainly not least, a word of praise for the artistry of photographers Geoff Goddard, Nigel Snowdon and Diana Burnett. Their craft is demonstrated by the outstanding photographs which play such an important part in the book. In a single frame they consistently capture the personalities of the sportsmen in this élite group – the Grand Prix winners.

Peter Lovering
Richmond, Surrey

Black and white photographs:
GODDARD PICTURE LIBRARY
NIGEL SNOWDON
DIANA BURNETT
MARLBORO WORLD CHAMPIONSHIP TEAM
LAT PHOTOGRAPHIC

Colour photographs:
GODDARD PICTURE LIBRARY
NIGEL SNOWDON
LAT PHOTOGRAPHIC

THE FIFTIES

By Denis Jenkinson

Froilan Gonzalez in the Ferrari defeats the works Alfa
Romeo team in the British Grand Prix in 1951.

KNOWN to his friends as 'Nino', Dr Farina had a long and successful career spanning the years 1934 to 1955, driving Alfa Romeo, Maserati and Ferrari cars as well as Tony Vandervell's Thinwall Special Ferrari. That Farina was a man of some substance, with a professional doctorate, was evident the moment you met him; he never really approved of workers, or *artisans*, becoming Grand Prix drivers, viewing the profession with a certain amount of pride and jealousy.

By 1937 Farina was a fully fledged member of the Alfa Romeo factory team run by the Scuderia Ferrari, but his skills did not reap their true reward as the Milanese cars were outpaced by the German Mercedes-Benz and Auto Union teams. None the less, Farina drove hard and fast. His driving was fearless and ruthless, and his character changed little when he was out of the cockpit (unlike some great drivers), although he could be charming and gracious when the occasion called for it. He was always master of his machinery, no matter what it was, but he was very hard on the mechanism – a car had to be strong to be driven by Farina. His 'laid-back' style, sitting well back from the steering wheel with arms at full stretch, had an almost regal air about it, in sharp contrast to most Grand Prix drivers of his day who tended to crouch over the wheel.

He won the last Grand Prix race to be held at Tripoli, driving a Tipo 158 Alfa Romeo, as Italy became embroiled in the European war in 1940. As soon as the war was over he reappeared with the Alfa Romeo factory team and was the pacesetter of the day. When Alfa Romeo withdrew for the 1949 season Farina drove for Ferrari and Maserati, and in 1950, when the FIA World Championship was introduced, Farina became the first official World Champion, winning the British GP, the Swiss GP and the Italian GP. Like many subsequent World Champions, he was not the best driver of his era when he won the title, but he was very competent at all times.

When Alfa Romeo finally withdrew in 1952, Farina joined the Scuderia Ferrari, but did not enjoy having to be number two to young Alberto Ascari. His innate pride was to be his downfall, for he became accident-prone through his inability to accept 'anno domini' and he could not ease up. In the 1954 Mille Miglia, when I came across the smoking wreck of Farina's 4.1-litre Ferrari smashed head-on into a tree soon after the start, it was no great surprise. He always managed to recover from his racing accidents and eventually retired in 1956, but died in a stupid road accident just ten years later.

The classic Farina style: on his way to victory in the 1950
British Grand Prix.

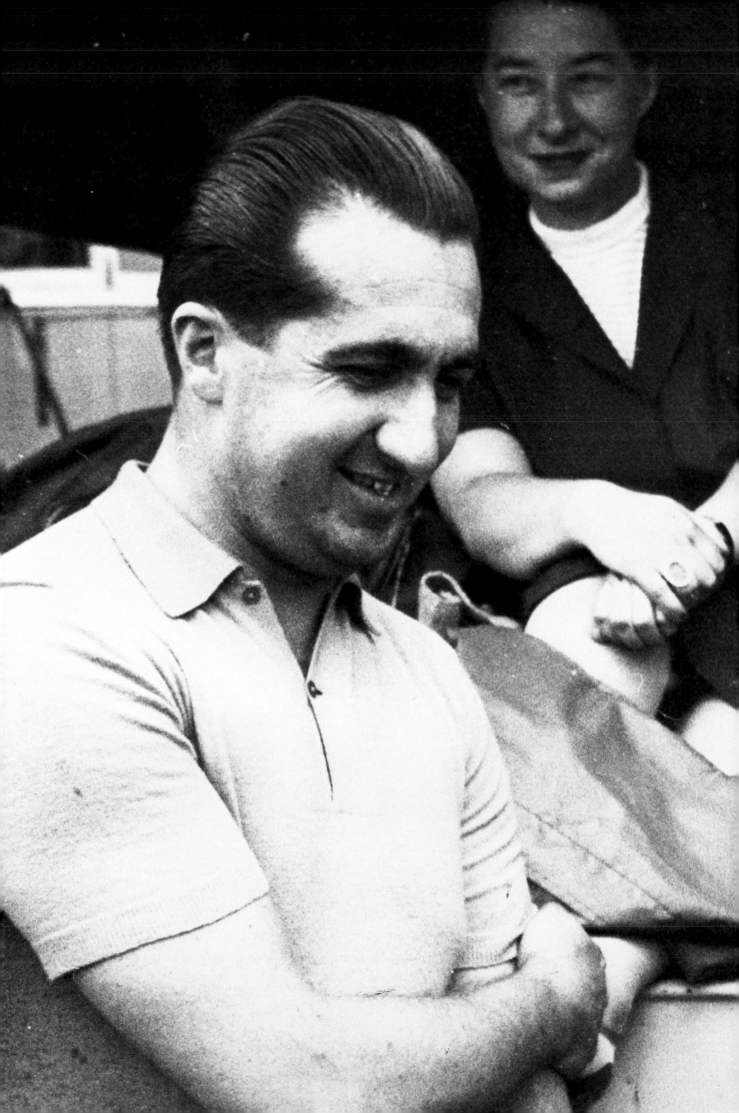

WITH such a famous father as Antonio Ascari, who was European Champion in 1925 driving for the Alfa Romeo team, young Alberto had a lot to live up to. Not only did he do this, but, in my estimation, he was the greatest Grand Prix driver of the 1950s. Perfection was his driving style, precise, accurate and unflustered. He seldom put a wheel wrong and his young team-mate in 1953, Mike Hawthorn, used to tell me what it was like to follow Ascari round a challenging circuit like Spa-Francorchamps. 'Bloody Ascari,' he would say, 'he is spot-on all the time and on every lap, there is never any variation.' This uncanny sense of judgement appeared everywhere in Ascari's driving, and never more so than at the start of a race. Photographs of starts in 1952 or 1953 invariably show a Ferrari way ahead on its own while most of the field are still controlling wheelspin. That will be Alberto Ascari.

Out of a racing car he was exactly the same: quiet and unruffled, nothing extrovert about his demeanour or behaviour; in fact, he was unobtrusive in the extreme. Being a racing driver was his chosen profession; it was not part of his family life, and he never encouraged his wife and family to accompany him, even to Monza, his local race track. This always struck me as strange, for Antonio had taken young Alberto to Monza when he was a small boy, as photos of him standing on the seat of an Alfa Romeo, with his father on one side and Enzo Ferrari on the other, testify. If he didn't win a Grand Prix you could imagine Alberto returning to his home in Milan, opening the door, embracing his wife and children, and saying 'I've had a bad day at the office – what do we have for supper tonight?'

Not only was Alberto a devout Roman Catholic but he was inordinately superstitious, which used to amuse Fangio, who was practical and pragmatic. But that is the way Ascari was. He had a horror of black cats, and driving through a town he would turn round and take another route rather than pass a black cat sitting on the pavement.

It was while I was motoring across the South of France in the summer of 1955 that I heard with total disbelief on my car radio of his death at an unofficial test day at Monza. The undisputed King of Grand Prix racing in 1952 and 1953 was dead, and only a week after he had survived a plunge into the harbour in a Lancia D50 during the Monaco Grand Prix. As the car sank to the bottom of the harbour we all felt that Alberto would surely drown, but he bobbed up to the surface and swam strongly to the rescue boat. Yet now he had died in an unexplainable crash in a borrowed sports Ferrari.

Ascari was almost unbeatable with the T500 Ferrari.
Here he wins the 1953 Belgian Grand Prix at Spa.

I F anyone had fire in his belly and a passion for racing it was the Argentinian 'Pepe' Gonzalez. His burly build and forceful, rather than elegant, driving style earned him the name 'II Cabezon' (the Pampas Bull). Gonzalez in a Ferrari or Maserati was not a pretty sight to watch, but it was very exciting, and it seemed to matter little to him whether his car was on the track or on the grass verge . . . his foot was always hard on the accelerator pedal. He was a great friend of Fangio, but on the track they were real rivals.

'Pepe' came to Europe with Fangio in 1950 to race in the Argentine-sponsored Maserati team, but it was not long before he was invited to join the Scuderia Ferrari. His finest hour was at Silverstone in the 1951 British Grand Prix when, driving a 4½-litre V12 Ferrari, he beat the all-conquering Alfa Romeo 159 team. While no-one had fought harder against him than Fangio, equally no-one was more pleased at this victory than his fellow countryman.

In 1955 he crashed in practice for the Tourist Trophy at Dundrod and although he raced again in his home country, for Europe the 'Pampas Bull' had been put out to grass.

I envy very few people in life, being well content with my own lifestyle, but one man I always envied was Piero Taruffi. A first-class motor cyclist, a brilliant engineer, a competent Grand Prix driver, he was above all a man who knew how to live a full and interesting life, encompassing everything from engineering through music to the arts – a man who enjoyed travel, fine living, had excellent taste in all things and a controlled passion for motor racing. He was an accomplished linguist with an exceptional brain, able to deal with all aspects of life and to extract the best from everything. An engineer/racing driver of the best type.

I would have loved to have ridden with him in the Mille Miglia, for his knowledge of the 1000-mile route was quite remarkable. He had the ability to drive any sort of racing car, but the pureness of the Grand Prix car appealed to the engineer in him. Although not a World Champion racing driver, he was a true Grand Prix driver and a born perfectionist in all things.

I N many people's eyes Juan Fangio was the greatest Grand Prix driver of all time; certainly, if results are how you judge greatness, then his record in Grand Prix racing will take some beating. Five times World Champion, using Alfa Romeo, Maserati, Mercedes-Benz and Ferrari cars, he won 24 of the 51 World Championship Grand Prix events which he contested. But Fangio was much more than a champion of statistics: he was a most likeable and friendly man, hard as nails in a Grand Prix car, yet gentle and *simpatico* out of the cockpit. He was shrewd when it came to business matters and had an uncanny foresight for choosing the teams for which he drove and the cars he used. However, he had his limitations as an all-round racing driver, showing little real interest in sports car racing, even though he drove in most of the big sports car events in the 1950s to fulfil contractual obligations.

He was born in Argentina in 1911 and raced in his own national events from 1934 to 1948, specialising in long-distance off-road marathons before turning to circuit racing with a home-made Chevrolet-engined single-seater. He made a brief foray to Europe in 1948, and in 1949 returned to make a full season of Grand Prix racing. He scored numerous victories and was so impressive that, despite his age (38), Alfa Romeo invited him to join their team of Tipo 158 'Alfettas'. With Alfa Romeo, his favourite make of racing car, he was World Champion in 1951, the first of his five championships.

He was admired and respected by all his contemporaries, especially the rising young stars who were quick to admit that 'the old man' was the greatest. If there was a fast corner that any of them could take nearly flat-out you could be sure that Fangio would take it absolutely flat-out. In later years when I asked him why he did things that the others could not or would not do, he replied simply: 'It was necessary; I was World Champion, and a true World Champion must always be the best.' He had the same philosophy about pole positions.

He was 47 years old when he retired from Grand Prix racing and he left behind him a legend that those of us who saw it in the making will cherish for all time. It was a great honour to know this remarkable man, who still carries with him that uncanny air of 'World Champion' wherever he appears. Young racing drivers of today still feel deep emotion when they meet this Grand Old Man of Grand Prix. The name itself is enough: Fangio – a true master of the art of Grand Prix racing and one who is respected the world over.

The maestro: Fangio drifts the Maserati 250F
through a bend.

HE was undoubtedly Britain's post-war wonder boy who could drive anything, anywhere at any time and always gave his maximum. He was a truly gifted artist at the wheel of a racing car who could even make bad cars look half-decent. He only knew one way to race and that was at 100 per cent; consequently his cars had to be strong, for if the car could give 100 per cent you knew that Stirling could use 110 per cent. It is doubtful whether any other driver has raced as great a variety of cars as he did, always excelling in whatever he drove. He worked 24 hours a day at being a professional racing driver for he reckoned that the paying public deserved to see him give of his best. Whether he was first or last he always put on a scintillating display of his skill and artistry.

He was one driver who was always ahead of his car's behaviour on the track, whereas others would be that fraction behind the car and its natural tendencies. Of the 66 World Championship Grand Prix races he contested he won 16, with 16 pole positions and 37 front row starts. His record in sports car racing was equally impressive, yet he was never crowned World Champion, and finished second four years in a row, three times behind Fangio and once behind Hawthorn.

If he had a fault it was his pride in being British, almost to the point of fanaticism; because of this he never joined the Scuderia Ferrari, who would have guaranteed him a World Championship. He got more pleasure out of racing for Rob Walker's private operation, a loner against the works teams, than he did in a factory team, even though he raced for HWM, Maserati, BRM and Vanwall. His exploits have filled many books, as have his escapes from racing accidents that were seldom his fault, but his career finally came to an end in 1962 with a crash at Goodwood.

He may not have been named a World Champion during his racing career from 1947 to 1962, but for me he was a World Champion driver, and the greatest all-rounder of his time. He was known in England as 'Mr Motor Racing', and justifiably so.

Spa 1958. Moss and Brooks in the Vanwalls lead the field
through Eau Rouge.

AS British as the Royal Family and roast beef, Mike was a 'super bloke'. He was a motoring enthusiast at heart, having developed the taste for fast cars and racing from his father, Leslie. I am a bit biased about Mike Hawthorn as I lived only a few miles from his Farnham home, but he was one of the few drivers I enjoyed meeting in the local pub for a beer or two and a chin-wag. If I called in to his father's garage in Farnham with an interesting car or motor cycle, his first words would be 'let's have a go', and away he would go, to return windswept and beaming with pleasure.

He didn't have the natural talent of Stirling Moss or Tony Brooks, but he made up for it by sheer enthusiasm and bravery. If he took me for a ride around a circuit I used to think, 'if I was brave enough, I could do what he is doing, but I know I don't have the bravery.' He could drive a sports car as well as he could drive a Grand Prix car, and one of his most memorable drives was in a D-type Jaguar in the Tourist Trophy at Dundrod in 1955. A Grand Prix that will remain in the memories of everyone who saw it was his battle against Fangio in 1953 at Reims, when he demonstrated clearly that a true-blue Englishman could take on the best and beat them. It was a great moment in Grand Prix history.

For many people, Mike's fetish for wearing a bow-tie while racing summed him up, but for me it was his 'flat 'at, pipe and pint of beer' when he wasn't racing that was the true Mike Hawthorn. His sense of fun at all times was natural and infectious. At one race, the prize-giving was upstairs in the town hall. We were all standing about in the foyer chatting when in came the fit and virile Stirling Moss, who bounded up the stairs two at a time and disappeared in a flash. Mike took the arm of his team-mate, Duncan Hamilton, and said, 'Come on Duncan, we'd better join him,' and in a splendid imitation of two very old men they helped each other up the stairs!

Mike's death in a road accident after he had retired from racing was tragic, but it was the result of his competitive spirit and willingness to 'have a go' at all times. I often think that Mike's last words before his Jaguar hit the tree must have been 'Oh F . . .'

Mike Hawthorn drives the Ferrari into third place at the
1957 British Grand Prix, Aintree.

product of the post-war 500 cc racing scene, Peter Collins soon demonstrated that he was capable of handling a lot more power than a motor cycle could provide. In quick leaps and bounds he was soon into serious racing, graduating from F2 HWM to the 400 horsepower of Mr Vandervell's Thinwall Special Ferrari. Aston Martin also gave him the opportunity to race in the long-distance classic races and inevitably he came to the notice of Ferrari, who took him into the Scuderia in 1956 with the Lancia-Ferrari V8 cars.

In the happy, carefree times of the 1950s a driver had the opportunity to race a large variety of cars in an equally varied choice of events, and Peter Collins did exactly that. He drove anything and everything, anywhere, thoroughly enjoying the casual life of the professional racing driver, even though his father's transport firm would have given him a steady job and good living.

He was not particularly popular with some team managers, as he had a tendency to 'lark about' if he felt the situation was not serious, but once in a racing car he settled down and drove in a hard and determined fashion, very similar in style to Mike Hawthorn, from whom he learnt a lot. Sadly, he crashed in the German GP at the Nürburgring in 1958, just in front of his chum Mike, and died shortly afterwards.

My lasting memory of Peter Collins was when I was on my way to the British Grand Prix at Aintree in my little Porsche 356. I drew up alongside a large articulated lorry at some traffic lights and realised the driver was hurling abuse down at me, the way lorry drivers can do. I looked up and there was Peter Collins grinning broadly from behind the wheel of the artic. He too, was on his way to Aintree and was delivering the lorry for his father as it was on his route.

Peter Collins, a favoured 'son' of Ferrari. His gesture in allowing Fangio to take his car at the 1956 Italian Grand Prix will never be forgotten at Maranello.

THE bearded Swede from the rich Stockholm family was not motivated by cars and racing so much as by the racing life, the travel, the good living and the international lifestyle. He was a very 'dry' character, with an aloof air and was not very outgoing. Although his English was near-perfect it did have that slightly Scandinavian ring to it, but he always spoke slowly and quietly, seldom showing any emotion, even under stress.

He won only one Grand Prix race, despite taking part in more than a hundred, always driving for factory teams after his first two seasons with his own Maserati. His victory came with BRM in the 1959 Dutch Grand Prix at Zandvoort, and I am sure he was as surprised about it as anyone.

Whereas the rough and ready racing characters like Fangio or Hawthorn never gave safety a first thought, let alone a second, drivers like Bonnier were more interested in living than in winning. It was ironic that his death at Le Mans came because the safety barriers were not high enough to stop his little Lola flying over them and into the trees.

WHEN I first saw Tony Brooks in action, he stood out head and shoulders above everyone else – not by reason of winning races, but by his poise and style of driving. The car was right on the limit of tyre adhesion, yet perfectly balanced and smooth, with the driver showing no signs of working hard or juggling with the situation. Clearly here was a man with a delicate touch, a fine sense of balance and a natural flair for speed. Tony's driving style complemented the evolution in racing car design. Being of slight build, he drove with his brain and his finger tips, rather than his arm muscles and a big heart. None the less, his passion for racing was all-absorbing.

I was lucky enough to be at the 1955 Syracuse Grand Prix when Tony trounced the works Maserati team, driving a Connaught. He did it in such an effortless manner that the organisers felt forced to have the Connaught engine dismantled to make sure it was not over the limit of 2½ litres. At that point few people had heard of Tony Brooks, but that all changed, for his association with the Vanwall team and later with the Scuderia Ferrari put him near the top of the Grand Prix tree.

The Cooper Years

THE nut-brown Brabham from Sydney, Australia, was the perfect example of a garage mechanic turned Grand Prix driver. He was not an engineer in the academic sense, but he was a gifted fettler and he knew exactly what he wanted of a racing car, even if others disagreed. He came to the European scene in the mid-1950s, knocking on people's doors to see if they wanted a racing driver. John Cooper, of Cooper Cars, decided he wanted one and a partnership started which culminated in Jack Brabham and Cooper winning the Formula 1 World Championship in 1959 and 1960.

He was a shrewd businessman and was the inspiration behind Cooper Cars' racing efforts. What Jack wanted Cooper gave him, with very satisfying results. I well recall talking to John Cooper one winter and asking about his Formula 1 car for the next season. He said, with all honesty, 'I can't tell you until Jack gets back from Australia.'

Jack's actual driving talent was nothing very special, but his knowledge of racing and track-craft was hard to beat. Coupled with his business sense, Jack's racing was very successful in more than results on paper. People would say that he would only really start going when he heard the cash register beginning to ring up the winnings – and they were not far wrong.

His ability to tune an engine and set up the chassis for what he wanted from the car was a natural gift and I had a long technical discussion with him one day when Cooper were just getting into Formula 1. He described to me in great detail just what he was aiming to achieve in the way of steering and handling, even though he could not explain the theory, and I found it fascinating to listen to him. Three years earlier I had had a similar discussion with the Daimler-Benz engineers on racing car design, except that they were explaining it to me mathematically. The end result of the two discussions was the same!

The real worth of Jack Brabham's stature in Grand Prix racing can be judged by the pleasure with which everyone sees him today when he turns up at a Grand Prix to see how things are going. One characteristic he has never lost is his use of one word in answer to a question when the questioner was hoping for a whole sentence! Taciturn, I think they call it.

Halcyon days, when Brabham and Cooper were a
dominant force in the 2½ litre formula.

MAURICE grew up amid racing and he was soon taking part in minor French events. When war broke out he stored his Bugatti in a barn in the family vineyards where, unknown to him, rats nested in the fuel tank. Once peace had returned, Maurice retrieved the car and entered for the first race in France in 1945. He retired with fuel lines choked by *petoulet*, the French slang for 'rat shit', which became his nickname. In fact, it was a real contradiction for he was always neat and immaculate, and he drove in the same way.

In the post-war years 'Petoulet' was one of the 'Three Musketeers', the trio of French drivers who did so much for the tittle Gordini team that strove valiantly to uphold French honour in Grand Prix racing. By 1954 Maurice had earned his way into the Ferrari works team, and later drove Rob Walker's Cooper-Climax. He stayed in Grand Prix racing a little too long, ending his career in 1964 in a private BRM team of not very high standards. However, in France he will always be remembered for the way he drove 'pour la patrie'.

HARRY SCHELL:
Playboy – the original
American in Paris.

JEAN BEHRA: Tiger.

LUIGI VILLORESI:
Grand old man.

LUIGI FAGIOLI:
Pre-war ace.

LUIGI MUSSO:
Very proud of Italy.

EUGENIO CASTELLOTTI:
Very proud of being an Italian.

ROY SALVADORI:
Aerodrome racer.

STUART LEWIS-EVANS *(centre)*:
A new era: brain before brawn.

THE SIXTIES

By Nigel Roebuck

Jochen Rindt in the Cooper-Maserati dives inside the
Ferrari of Chris Amon at La Source hairpin, 1967 Belgian
Grand Prix.

GIVEN his time over again, Phil Hill says he would never be a racing driver. And to suggest that a career second time around could work out so well is probably stretching credibility too far. In nearly 20 years of racing, Hill won the World Championship, the Le Mans 24 Hours three times, as well as countless other races – and never once was he hurt. No-one can reasonably ask more than that.

Phil, in fact, was a racing driver in spite of himself. Introspective and edgy before a race, he would pace up and down, lighting one cigarette after another, like a man on Death Row. But once in the car, once under way, the nerves calmed, doubts disappeared; his style became easy and composed. He was one of those, like Brooks or Rodriguez or Ickx, who excelled at the unyielding circuits. And he shone, too, in treacherous conditions.

For years the quiet Californian had his sights on Formula 1, but Enzo Ferrari considered him a sports car driver. Only when Musso and Collins were killed within a month of each other, in the summer of 1958, was Phil brought in to partner Hawthorn at Monza. In a sensational debut, he led much of the way, and his Grand Prix future was assured.

Perhaps he was at his greatest in 1960, when Ferrari – still front-engined – were outclassed on all but the very fastest circuits. In the beautiful Dino 246 Phil took a miraculous third at Monaco, pressured Brabham hard at Spa, shone at Oporto, finally won at Monza.

Hill's time truly came the following year, when only he and Ferrari team-mate von Trips were in serious contention for the World Championship. And Phil clinched the title at Monza in the most sorrowful circumstances imaginable. Taffy had been killed early in the race, and on the rostrum the face of America's first World Champion was drawn, eyes glazed.

Perhaps he should have retired at that point. Certainly his friends thought so. But Hill was firmly wedded to his way of life by now, had grown accustomed to the ways of Italy, where he could indulge his passion for music, go to La Scala in Milan whenever he chose.

It is doubtful that anyone more intelligent than this gentle and perceptive man has ever sat in a racing car. At the end of 1967 he felt that enough was enough, slipped back to the West Coast, got married, relaxed at last.

Phil Hill's 1961 World Championship was the pinnacle of
his career, though he will be remembered by many as one
of sports car racing's greatest drivers.

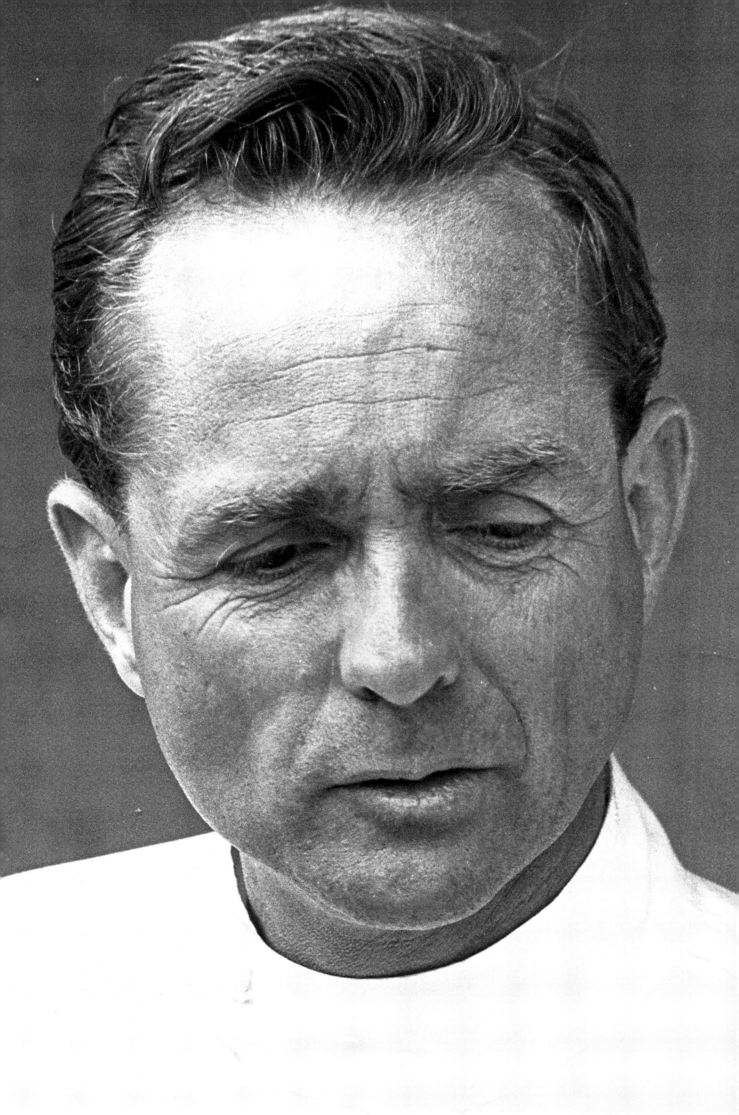

COUNT von Trips was a gentleman in the real sense of the word, and he raced cars because he had a passion for it. Ferrari loved him for his courteous manners and humour, and also for his utter fearlessness. The Old Man's favourites were always abnormally brave.

For most of his career von Trips was confined largely to sports car racing. Occasional Formula 1 drives left no doubts that he was quick enough, but there were several huge accidents, and it was not until 1960 that Ferrari gave him a permanent place in the Grand Prix team.

All he knew about cars was how to drive them, and in those days that was how they liked their drivers at Maranello. 'Leave the technical stuff to us' was their maxim, and Taffy was only too happy to comply.

In 1961 the Ferrari 156, with classic 'sharknose' profile, was the thing to have, and at last it all looked to be coming right for von Trips. He won at Zandvoort, took another fine victory at Aintree in the rain, scored well everywhere. Leading the World Championship from team-mate Phil Hill, he went to Monza, took pole position. And on the second lap, after a touch with Clark, he went off the road and was killed instantly.

ON a wet afternoon at Aintree, in July 1961, Giancarlo Baghetti's shark-nose Ferrari spun and slid off the road, hitting a fence. An extraordinary sequence of events had come to an end. The Italian had come to the British Grand Prix with an unbeaten record: three races, three wins.

Baghetti's Grand Prix career, although brief, was remarkable. In March 1961 he drove a Ferrari in his first Formula 1 race, at Siracusa, and won it, after a battle with Gurney's Porsche. Two months later came his second event, in Naples, and that he also took. Finally, in July, he took part in his first Grande Epreuve, the French Grand Prix at Reims. And, astoundingly, that race, too, ended in dramatic victory for him – again over Gurney.

That, though, was the long and short of it. Afterwards Giancarlo never did anything worth a damn in Formula 1. He had a full season with Ferrari in '62, moved to the calamitous ATS team the following year, and after that took rides as and when they cropped up. A sort of lesser Scarfiotti, he was a charming fellow, of considerable wealth, who slipped out of racing quietly. It had been, in effect, a career in reverse.

RICHIE Ginther was the perfect second driver. Although he had great days in his F1 career, he was never consistently on a par with Clark, Hill or Gurney. He knew it and accepted it, as honest with himself as with others.

For all that, he was more than a journeyman and this tiny Californian was rarely far off the absolute pace. While leading the 1961 French Grand Prix at Reims, he felt the engine beginning to tighten up, and so he came in, parked the car, walked away. The Ferrari mechanics could not believe it, but that was Ginther: he hated to abuse machinery.

This extraordinary mechanical sympathy, quite untypical of the era, made him a fine test driver and he was used to great effect by Ferrari and BRM. When Honda got serious about Formula 1, in 1965, Richie was the perfect choice to lead the team and he won with the Japanese car in Mexico – the last race of the 1500 cc Formula 1.

In 1967 he briefly partnered Gurney in the Eagle-Weslakes, then, quite out of the blue, told Dan he wanted to stop. Simply, he felt the time was right, and he never drove a race car again.

I RELAND was born ten years too late. With his attitude to racing he should have been a Grand Prix driver through the Fifties, a colleague of Collins, Hawthorn and Schell. His style belonged in a Maserati 250F. As it was, he arrived at a time of transition, when engines were moving behind the driver, when drivers were spending less time behind the bar.

After occasional Lotus drives in 1959, Ireland fairly burst upon the GP scene early in 1960, winning at both Goodwood and Silverstone in Chapman's rear-engined 18. Later that year, he led Moss and Brabham at Oulton Park, went off the road and repassed them within a few laps.

Innes was very quick, had a lot of accidents over the years, and was always prepared to run at the limit. His last-lap victory over the Porsches at Solitude in 1961 was unforgettable. Later the same year, at Watkins Glen, he scored Team Lotus's first Grand Prix victory, but soon afterwards Chapman decided that Ireland no longer figured in his plans. It was too late to find another competitive ride, and sadly Innes never again drove for a top team.

AFTER Clark's death, in early 1968, Chris Amon eloquently summed up the feelings of the drivers: 'Beyond the grief, there was also a fear which we all felt. If it could happen to him, what chance did the rest of us have? It seemed we'd lost our leader . . .'

After Moss's enforced retirement in 1962, Jim swiftly and quite naturally took over as the yardstick by which others were judged, and perhaps no racing driver in history has dominated an era quite as he did. It may be argued that racing was less competitive in his time than now, and certainly the Lotus was usually the best car. But beyond dispute, too, is that he was by a league the best of his time – perhaps the best of any time.

Consider the bare statistics of those eight Formula 1 seasons: 25 wins, 33 pole positions, 27 fastest laps . . . and all from 72 starts. But the single fact which tells most about Clark is that only once did he finish second. In other words, if he made it to the flag, he invariably made it before anyone else.

It seems inappropriate that history tends to shackle Jim's memory to the 1.5-litre era, for these were hardly Grand Prix cars for the Gods. And the truth is that, whatever the regulations of his time, the quietly spoken Scot would have ruled. He had it all.

Clark's entire character changed when he got into a racing car. Outside it, he was a nervous man for most of his life. Only in his last years did he come to realise, and accept, his status, becoming more confident and worldly. But he never stopped biting his nails, and he shrank from making speeches.

Usually he was courteous, kind, wry. And his pure love of motor racing was beyond question; money was always a secondary consideration. He would have detested the sport as it is today, with commercialism rampant, PR persons at every turn. Jim Clark was a man of action, not words. A man to whom races seemed to surrender, one who, like Ascari, won by imperious command. A man who, in 1967, took pole position at the Nürburgring by *nine* seconds and more.

That was his last full season, and we saw him at his greatest, which was very great indeed. No mannerly Lotus 25, this. It was the 49, with prototype Cosworth DFV engine, a wayward package which had to be fought. Four times he won with it that year, and another in his last Grand Prix, at Kyalami early in 1968, brought the tally up to 25. Without that tyre failure at grey and rainy Hockenheim on 7 April, who knows what kind of figure his successors might have faced? Jim was 32 and at his zenith.

In the hands of Jim Clark the Lotus 49 was uncatchable.
He led every Grand Prix for which they were entered and
only unreliability denied him the 1967 World
Championship.

'HE'S a Graham Hill' has become over the years a Formula 1 catchphrase to describe any driver whose success apparently owes more to guts and determination than to natural ability. During the Sixties Clark and Gurney were regarded as the naturals, Hill the worker who got there by application and sweat. And Graham would bristle at that.

It was, of course, all relative. No man entirely devoid of raw talent could have won the World Championship (twice), the Indianapolis 500 and the Le Mans 24 Hours. And what of five victories in the Monaco Grand Prix?

Some might argue that Graham's need to work, to practise, to calculate, makes his success the more admirable. With no family wealth to support him, he worked his passage into motor racing, trading his services as a mechanic for the odd drive. It was this tactic which got him into Team Lotus.

The meat of Hill's career, though, was spent at BRM, 10 of his 14 Grand Prix victories being won between 1962 and 1965. After seven years there he returned to Lotus, and the real quality of the man was never more apparent than in 1968, following the death of Clark.

Jimmy had *been* Team Lotus, yet somehow, in the dreadful aftermath of Hockenheim, Graham kept Chapman and his men together, strengthened their resolve, made them start again. At Jarama, the first race without Clark, Hill won. Then came Monte Carlo, and he won there, too. At 39, he was telling them that he was ready to be World Champion again.

After his huge accident at Watkins Glen in 1969, in which he severely injured his legs, many would have been happy to see Graham quit. He was 40, and had done it all. But retiring in those circumstances was not the man's way. There was something to conquer here, and so he conquered it. He even won again, at the International Trophy in 1971 for Brabham, and at Le Mans the following year for Matra.

In 1973 he formed his own team, and his last two seasons were a sad embarrassment to all who had seen him at his peak. Especially poignant was the sight of him climbing from his car at Monaco in 1975, having failed to qualify for this, the race he had made his own. He never drove again.

When he died, along with members of his team, that freezing November night, there was enormous grief at the news. Graham was held in affection by people who had never been near a race circuit. His personality and humour had taken him beyond his own immediate sphere. And now a national institution had been lost.

After the loss of Clark at Hockenheim Graham Hill rallied the Lotus team with victories at Jarama and Monaco *(above)*. This second World Championship in 1968 was universally popular.

THE tragedy of John Surtees is that people tend to remember him as the Formula 1 constructor who failed, who left the sport a disillusioned man. Often overlooked is his greatness as a racing driver.

And he was great. The transition from bikes to cars was made with barely a break in stride. In June of 1960 he dominated TT week on the MV Agusta, and the following month drove a Lotus to second place in the British Grand Prix. By mid-August, in Portugal, he had the car on pole position and ran away with the race until retirement. Other Lotus drivers at Oporto included Moss and Clark . . .

The Ferrari years produced one World Championship, in 1964, and there would surely have been a second, two years later, had not driver and team split at mid-season.

Throughout his career Surtees never learned diplomacy, which is another way of saying that old-fashioned qualities like adherence to principle still counted with him. He always spoke his mind, a quality scarcely universal in Grand Prix racing, and sometimes he did it witheringly. In truth, he never fitted in as comfortably as he had in the less 'precious' motor cycle world.

Two years with Honda brought out the best and worst in John. His dedication to the project was unflagging, and many times he had the heavy and wilful V12 into places it had no business to be. At Monza in 1967 he even won with it. But the enthusiasm was ground away by frustration with the slow-moving Japanese. It was a partnership which should have produced more.

A season with BRM, in 1969, was worse, far worse, to the point that he can hardly bring himself to discuss it even today. After that he decided to follow the example of Brabham and McLaren, to form his own team. At the end of 1971 he retired as a driver.

Had Surtees been content merely to drive, who knows what he might have achieved? Although he would often stress that he was not an engineer, too often he tried to behave like one. This, wherever he went, caused friction, and inevitably took a toll of his driving. No-one can do it all.

At his best, John was a racer of the purest kind, a driver of deftness and enormous courage, exactly the fellow to shine at Spa in the wet. In hindsight he seems invariably to have chosen the difficult route. But he probably wouldn't agree . . .

A superb photograph of Surtees and the Honda on the
limit at the 1967 British Grand Prix.

FOR Lorenzo Bandini, Grand Prix racing *was* Ferrari. The notion of driving for anyone else would have been inconceivable, and there can be little doubt that he raced at least as much for the old man of Maranello as for himself. Through his years of childhood poverty, he had dreamed only of becoming a Ferrari driver.

The sadness was that Lorenzo never made it to the summit. He was a fine driver, sometimes a brilliant one, but never great. Only in the last few months of his life were there signs of fully realising all that early potential.

He won only once, at Zeltweg in 1964, but there should have been more. For most of his career at Ferrari, he was a loyal number two to Surtees, but for 1967 was finally and unequivocally *numero uno*. At Monte Carlo he qualified on the front row, led at the start, and in the late stages was chasing Hulme when he crashed appallingly at the chicane. Terribly burned, he died three days later. Bandini's accident, seen on television screens across the world, had a massive effect on the future of racing safety, but that was of little consolation in Italy, which mourned the loss of a favourite son.

S CARFIOTTI is one of those anomalies who must inevitably find their way into a book of this kind. It is ironic that Chris Amon, one of his Ferrari team-mates in the Sixties, and an incomparably greater driver, is absent because somehow he never did win a Grand Prix. But 'Lulu' did, and it came at the best possible place – Monza. The 1966 Italian was one of only ten Grands Prix in which he competed.

Grandson of the first president of Fiat, cousin of Gianni Agnelli, Scarfiotti was born into extraordinary wealth. His life could have been one of carelessness and ease, and it was perhaps this which drove him to seek a means of testing himself. A man of humour and debonair charm, he developed into a magnificent sports car driver, but the dream was always Formula 1.

Ferrari, though, believed it beyond Scarfiotti. Despite the impressive Monza victory, there were only a couple of drives afterwards. Ludovico, assuredly the last of the true gentleman racers, signed Cooper and Porsche contracts for 1968, and it was in one of the German sports cars that he lost his life, practising at the Rossfeld hill climb in June.

DAN Gurney never won the World Championship, nor even came close. Yet he was the rival most truly feared by Clark, and it seems barely credible that the man who was perhaps the greatest American Grand Prix driver ever took only four victories from all those years.

The classic circuits always drew out the best in him, and perhaps Spa-Francorchamps was his favourite. In 1964 he and the Brabham were in their own class there, on the pole and in front all the way until the last lap, when the fuel ran out. Fittingly, though, Gurney's only Grand Prix win in his own gorgeous Eagle-Weslake came at Spa three years later.

There were those who claimed Dan to be hard on his cars, and it is undeniable that he was known actually to have broken the gear lever, even the steering wheel, in the course of a race. But his style in the race car was as relaxed as his manner out of it. A delightful man, he never got bitter, never lost his humour or zest, however frequently his cards came from the bottom of the pack. He had a feel for the roots of motor racing; you watched his face during a demonstration by Fangio and you saw a schoolboy's enthusiasm, untouched by the hostile Fates.

McLAREN was never going to die in a racing car, just as Nuvolari would never live to retire. Yet the Italian succumbed to tuberculosis at 61, and Bruce was killed in a freak accident, testing at Goodwood on a Tuesday afternoon.

As a Formula 1 driver, he is difficult to place. More than a mere journeyman, he was never in the first rank. You looked to McLaren to take thirds and fourths, to score points consistently. Yet when the mood took him – as at the Race of Champions in 1968 – he could be devastating, and he remains the youngest man ever to win a Grand Prix. He was just 22 when he took the flag at Sebring in late 1959.

A modest and friendly man, Bruce seemed to carry his personality with him into a Grand Prix race: winning was not *that* important. You rarely saw him truly chance his arm. When his own F1 team got properly under way, in '68, he was quite content to play second driver to Hulme.

You sensed, too, that retirement was not far away. The future was McLaren Cars. The company: that was what brought his real ambition into play. As a driver, Bruce never had the ego so essential to stars; long-term what he wanted was to direct.

The Brabham Years

I N Europe Brabham was never a man to capture the public imagination. Quiet and undemonstrative, he never used two words where one would do, never became 'worldly'. Travelling constantly brought its own problems, and he would take steaks out from England with him, wary of the effects of foreign food. He was one of the first drivers to fly to races in his own aeroplane, and it must amuse him that now it is *de rigueur* among the fashionable. Jack kept to himself. It was no matter of being unfriendly; simply, he was an introvert.

On the track, though, it was a different matter. There was nothing shy about Jack Brabham, racing driver. His apprenticeship, served on the dirt ovals of New South Wales, had been rough and tumble, and Black Jack knew every trick in the book. Some said he wrote the book. Time and again one of his rear wheels would edge off the road, pepper those behind with gravel and dirt. He came of a hard school, and accepted the knocks as he handed them out. And at the end of the race there was inevitably that innocent flicker of a smile. Who, me?

Brabham was a doughty competitor. His style – shoulders hunched, head down – was never elegant, but in full cry he was a mighty impressive sight.

As he pioneered private flying among the drivers, so Jack was also the first to form his own team. The early Cooper years had been wonderful, bringing back-to-back World Championships, but later his horizons changed, and the first F1 Brabham appeared at the German Grand Prix in 1962.

For the next three seasons he was happy enough to be number two, in his own team, to Dan Gurney. But in 1966 Jack began a memorable Indian summer. In this, the first year of the new 3-litre Formula 1, the team's Repco engines were not to the forefront on horsepower, but what they had they gave for ever. At Reims, nearly six years after his last victory, Brabham became the first man to win a Grand Prix in a car bearing his own name. He also took the next three races – and his third title.

To the end of his career, Jack was always a factor. In his final season, 1970, he had one win and should have had several more. In Mexico, his last race, the Ferraris were beyond reach, but when he retired Brabham was running third. At 44, he was still in there, still pitching.

Brabham at the 1966 German Grand Prix.

DENIS Clive Hulme was one of history's more unlikely World Champions. Surely no-one that laid back could have made it to the pinnacle? But Denny did.

He was, by his own admission, a lazy fellow, his entire approach to life always a matter of taking the simplest, most direct route. Denny disliked uncertainties, making a point, for example, of staying in Holiday Inns whenever possible. Buenos Aires or Berlin, they were all exactly the same, and that was what he liked about them.

Similarly, Hulme liked to have everything weighed up on the race track. Like Scheckter, he never saw Formula 1 remotely as a romantic thing. Paramount in both their minds was survival: if it were wet during practice, very well, Denny sat the session out. After all, the rain always stopped eventually, didn't it?

In the quest to improve safety in Grand Prix racing, the New Zealander contributed more than anyone save Stewart. Behind the gruff and sometimes intimidating public face there was a sensitive man, deeply affected by tragedy in the sport. It was the manner of Peter Revson's death, in 1974, which determined Denny to quit once and for all.

This sells short his career, however. You could have got spectacular odds on Hulme for the World Championship in 1967. With but a season and a bit of Formula 1 behind him, he and the Brabham scarcely looked a serious rival for Clark, Hill and so on. True enough, he won only twice that year, but they were prestigious victories, at Monte Carlo and the Nürburgring. And, when they added up the points, he had more than anyone else.

It was typical of Denny that by then he had already decided to change teams; Bruce McLaren was mounting a serious Formula 1 effort for 1968. Hulme liked the look of it, and Bruce was a friend. QED, mate.

To the end of his career, Denny remained a McLaren driver. Perhaps he coasted through his final season, but until then he was never to be discounted. Once in a while, as at Kyalami in 1971, he was simply the fastest man in the place. And when victory was a real possibility, Hulme could, and would, race with anyone. During the closing laps at Anderstorp in 1973 he switched off the rev limiter, got his head down and passed the ailing Peterson with a couple of laps to go.

And it all ended quietly, just as he would have wished. Four laps into the US Grand Prix of 1974 Denny's engine blew. Yes, he smilingly said, that was it, finish. Now it was back to New Zealand, health and humour intact.

Denny Hulme: a greatly underrated driver who shone in
all types of racing. His World Championship in 1967 was
with Brabham, but he moved on to become a key figure in
the McLaren team.

JOCHEN Rindt . . . what do we remember of him? The mesmeric car control, the deep, clipped voice, the boxer's nose, tousled hair. And we who saw him, perhaps we recall the swell of sound from the grandstands which greeted his approach on one of the great days.

In every era there should be someone like Jochen, someone to bring a race to life, make it crackle. Ronnie was another such, Gilles perhaps the most extreme example of all. Each won races in cars which had no business winning races. It rarely happens, but when it does, the day inevitably passes into legend.

Rindt's early career gave no hint of the greatness to come. As a Formula Junior driver in the early Sixties he was remarkable only for flamboyant dress and a loud mouth, but once into Formula 2 he swiftly asserted himself. In Grand Prix racing, though, three seasons with Cooper and one with Brabham yielded little. Jochen's Formula 1 career began to flourish only when he joined Lotus in 1969.

It was a year of highs and lows. The Austrian quickly established himself as Stewart's only serious rival, but through most of the season Lotus reliability was wretched. Colin Chapman, fearful of losing Jochen, spoke of the revolutionary car he had planned for 1970, promised him absolute priority within the team. Rindt was persuaded, and at Watkins Glen finally won his first Grand Prix. It had been no better than any of his drives that year, he said. For once the car had stayed together.

As Chapman had promised, the new Lotus 72 made everything else obsolete. In 1970 Jochen won consecutively at Zandvoort, Clermont Ferrand, Brands Hatch and Hockenheim. Before these, however, had come a win at Monaco in the old 49, and this was Rindt's day of days. Even now, these many years later, people stand in Casino Square and recall that May afternoon. For Jochen the merest scent of victory was enough, and in the closing laps he showed them genius as he chased Brabham.

Often arrogant and intolerant of fools, he wasn't for everyone. Yet he had about him, too, a vulnerability. Through that last summer he worried that suddenly everything was going almost too well for him. The others were having the bad luck; the title was as good as won.

He lost his life during the final qualifying session at Monza, when 'something broke' on the Lotus 72. He is recorded in the history books as the only posthumous World Champion. Those who saw him, though, remember Jochen chiefly for this: he made them catch their breath.

Rindt in typical shape with the Lotus 72, a car which at
last allowed him to fulfil his potential but in which he
was tragically to lose his life.

HRONOMATIC
HEUER

T HINK of Seppi, and you remember first a fearlessness that could be chill-
ing. You watched him, and often you feared for him; there was a streak of
wildness there, and the limits seemed fuzzy, ill-defined.

A gentle fellow, with a fine sense of humour, Siffert was popular with the other
drivers, but some were wary of him during working hours, running wheel to wheel
at, say, Monza. In these circumstances, Stewart would say, Seppi rather tended to
live for the moment.

He was never a polished Grand Prix driver, in the Lauda sense of the word,
never one to give his cars an easy time. Often he was over kerbs, brushing banks,
sideways. There were others of greater natural gift, who perhaps needed to give less
of themselves, but after every race in which he drove, you knew that Siffert had
been at the limit. That was the man. His background was the poorest of the poor,
but his love of racing, his commitment to it, took him finally into Formula 1.

We remember Siffert chiefly for his days in the Rob Walker Lotus 49, but in
1971 he joined BRM, heroically taking over the team leadership after the death of
Rodriguez. Only three months later Seppi, too, was gone.

HE was a fatalist, Pedro, a man who believed absolutely that God called the shots. His philosophy was always evident in his driving, at once stylish and fearless. Rodriguez, child of arid Mexico, was never better than in treacherous and uncertain conditions.

Driving sports cars for John Wyer, and with BRM in Formula 1, Pedro settled happily in England. When he arrived at a circuit, it was in a sedately driven Bentley, and on his swept-back black hair sat a Bond Street deerstalker. But once into overalls, there was no hint of the dilettante. No-one raced harder than Rodriguez, and his stamina was a legend.

Spa-Francorchamps (the old circuit, of course) brought out every great quality in him. Amon, who tailed him throughout the Belgian Grand Prix of 1970, reported that his precision through the fast sweepers was absolute. Through history Pedro's name will be synonymous with the Porsche 917, but this day in the V12 BRM was his greatest.

It was his passion for the sport which killed him. A weekend without a race was a weekend lost, so he accepted an Interserie sports car drive at the Norisring in July 1971. And there he died by someone else's error.

The Sixties

THE most immediately evident feature of Jackie Stewart was his confidence. It was in everything he did, and right from the beginning. After a stunning F3 season with Ken Tyrrell in 1964, he had the choice of Lotus or BRM – the blue riband rides of the time – for his Formula 1 debut the following year. And here came early signs of a man who knew precisely where he was going.

Most attractive on paper had to be the Lotus drive. It was the fastest car in Grand Prix racing, and would have made Stewart team-mate to Jim Clark, a man he revered. But Jackie considered: this was a team which quite properly concentrated its energies on Clark. The number two Lotus, by legend, rarely made the finish. As well as that, Colin Chapman was a man who demanded results – and quickly. Better, Stewart reasoned, to do without that kind of pressure in his first season, to accept a sound, competitive car from BRM, learn from team leader Graham Hill and play himself in.

It was the right course to follow. After only a few races he had the measure of Hill, and swiftly emerged as the natural rival to Clark. At Monza he took the first of his 27 Grand Prix victories.

In 1966 he began with a top-drawer win in Monte Carlo, but at Spa came an accident he was fortunate to survive. It was to change fundamentally and for ever racing's traditionally *laissez-faire* attitude to safety. Trapped in the inverted car for several minutes, Stewart was soaked in fuel. He had a long time to be frightened, and thereafter cared not whom he upset: he was going to make racing as safe as it could reasonably be. Every Grand Prix driver of the last twenty-five years is in his debt.

After Clark's death, in early 1968, Jackie took over as The Man. Driving a Matra-Cosworth for Ken Tyrrell, he won three times that year, including that unforgettable day in the rain and drear at the Nürburgring. Second man Hill was more than four minutes behind . . .

There were six wins in 1969, easily enough to carry JYS to his first World Championship at the wheel of the Matra MS80, which stands to this day as his favourite car. He won that title as Clark would have won it: all ease and precision and sublime confidence, his place in the sport now beyond reasonable argument.

Jackie Stewart's Matra rounds the Station hairpin at Monaco, 1969. Although he retired from this race, six victories at other Grands Prix secured his first World Championship.

J ACKY Ickx was the prodigy of the time, the one for whom all things seemed possible. This was the man who qualified third at the Nürburgring in 1967 – in a Formula 2 Matra – the man whose fearless antics in that race had Stewart begging Ken Tyrrell to slow him down before he hurt himself. His apprenticeship was fiery.

And yet he matured into one of racing's true artists, with an effortless and fluent style. It was no surprise that the unsubtle technique required by ground-effect cars did not suit him. History will remember Jacky primarily as a sports car driver, which is sad and does him no justice. There were days in Formula 1 when he simply left everyone standing, and probably there has never been anyone better in the wet.

He was always an individualist. Testing bored him, and so, essentially, did competition. He would tell you, in that gravelly voice, that he always drove as if alone on the track, and he hoped it was faster than the others. The pleasure lay there, in seeing what was possible, in the battle between Ickx and himself.

WILLY MAIRESSE:
Always over the top.

MIKE PARKES:
Briefly impressive.

RICARDO RODRIGUEZ:
The genius of youth.

CHRIS AMON:
All talent, no luck.

DICKIE ATTWOOD:
Reliable journeyman.

MIKE SPENCE:
On the verge of the big time.

PIERS COURAGE:
By name and nature.

JOHNNY SERVOZ-GAVIN:
Gallic flair was not enough.

JACKIE OLIVER:
Never front rank.

TREVOR TAYLOR:
Yorkshire grit personified.

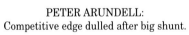

PETER ARUNDELL:
Competitive edge dulled after big shunt.

TONY MAGGS:
Always a number two.

The undisputed master in the Fifties, Juan Manuel
Fangio, drives the Mercedes-Benz W196 in the 1954
Spanish Grand Prix. His total of five World
Championships is unlikely to be surpassed.

The 1958 season was a tragic one for Scuderia Ferrari, Peter Collins and Luigi Musso losing their lives in accidents. Mike Hawthorn, seen here at the Belgian Grand Prix, wrested the drivers' championship from the grasp of Moss by his consistent performances. Within months, Britain's first World Champion was also dead, the victim of a road accident.

Though inevitably somewhat overshadowed by Stirling Moss, Tony Brooks was a hugely gifted driver who excelled on high-speed circuits, notching victories at Spa, the Nürburgring and AVUS. *Right:* Brooks is shown in the Vanwall in the early stages of the 1957 British Grand Prix at Aintree. Still not fully fit after a recent accident at Le Mans, Tony gave up his mount in mid-race to team-mate Moss, who took the car on to victory.

Jack Brabham and Cooper led the rear-engined revolution; World Championships in 1959 and 1960 were their reward. His win in the 1960 Belgian Grand Prix *(right)* was just one of five successive victories that season.

Only Stirling Moss could challenge the might of Ferrari in 1961; his victories at Monaco and the Nürburgring *(left)* with Rob Walker's Lotus rank among Grand Prix racing's greatest drives.

American Phil Hill took the 1961 drivers' title after his closest rival and Ferrari team-mate Wolfgang von Trips was killed at Monza. This cast a shadow over what had hitherto been a triumphant season for Maranello. Hill is pictured here taking the 'sharknose' Ferrari 156 V6 to third place in the Monaco Grand Prix.

In 1962 BRM at last fulfilled their potential and Graham Hill deservedly won the World Championship. His first-ever Grand Prix victory came at Zandvoort.

Jim Clark and Lotus were synonymous: two World Championships were scant reward for his efforts, for 33 pole positions, 25 wins, 27 fastest laps and 274 points were achieved from just 72 starts.
Below: Clark on his way to victory in the 1963 French Grand Prix at Reims.

John Surtees – the only champion on both two wheels and four – snatched the title for Ferrari in 1964. This superb photo shows him at work in the Monaco Grand Prix the following season.

Jackie Stewart's record-breaking Grand Prix career began with BRM in 1965. The Scot *(nearest camera)* started the British Grand Prix at Silverstone from the outside of the front row alongside Richie Ginther, Graham Hill and eventual winner Jim Clark, who dominated the World Championship with a total of six victories.

Richie Ginther scored the only Grand Prix win of his worthy career in Mexico in 1965. This race is best remembered as the first to be won on Goodyear tyres, but the Honda driver had also led in Holland *(right)*.

At the age of 40 Jack Brabham won the 1966 World Championship with a car built by his own team, a unique achievement. He is pictured cruising to victory in the Dutch Grand Prix.

It was the turn of Brabham's team-mate, New
Zealander Denny Hulme, to take the title in 1967.
The reliable Brabham-Repco failed to finish only twice
and gave Hulme victories at Monaco *(above)* and
the Nürburgring.

All eyes focus on the flag held aloft by the starter as
he prepares to unleash the pack at the start of the
1967 German Grand Prix. Clark's Lotus *(on the left)* is
on pole position, with Denny Hulme (Brabham),
Jackie Stewart (BRM) and Dan Gurney (Eagle)
completing the front row. Clark will retire, handing
victory to Hulme, the eventual World Champion.

Jim Clark gave the Ford-powered Lotus 49 a dream
debut at the 1967 Dutch Grand Prix *(above right)*,
winning as he pleased after team-mate Graham Hill
had succumbed to mechanical problems, but
unreliability would wreck his title challenge.

The revered Scot lost his life in a Formula 2 race early
the following season, but Hill took the 49, garishly
reliveried in deference to the team's new sponsor, to a
timely victory in the Spanish Grand Prix a month
later *(right)* and went on to claim his second
drivers' championship.

Jackie Stewart amassed a record of 27 Grand Prix
wins and three World Championships in a glittering
career. Victory in the 1969 Italian Grand Prix at
Monza in Ken Tyrrell's Matra-Ford *(top)* gave
him his first title.

Jochen Rindt *(above)* became the sport's first
posthumous World Champion after he was killed in
practice for the 1970 Italian Grand Prix. He is seen
struggling with the unsorted Lotus 72 at the Spanish
Grand Prix earlier in the season.

Jackie Stewart hurls his Tyrrell-Ford towards victory
in the 1971 British Grand Prix. The Scot was almost
unchallenged as he strode to his second World
Championship in three years.

Two years after it had taken Jochen Rindt to the
World Championship, the Lotus 72, now revised and
reliveried, was still good enough to give brilliant
young Brazilian Emerson Fittipaldi his first title.

Health problems wrecked Jackie Stewart's title
chances in 1972 but the supremely professional Scot
bounced back a year later to claim his third World
Championship. His victory at Monaco *(above right)*
was the 25th of his career, equalling the record
established by Jim Clark, and by the time he
retired at the end of the season he had added
two more to his total.

A switch to McLaren brought Emerson Fittipaldi
(right) his second World Championship in 1974, the
Brazilian's consistency and tactical awareness giving
him the edge over the faster Ferraris.

Overleaf: The 1975 World Champion, Niki Lauda,
triumphed again in 1977, his skill and courage
against the odds marking him as a true great.
Here, 'Super Rat' heads for victory in the
Dutch Grand Prix at Zandvoort.

THE SEVENTIES

By Alan Henry

Ronnie Peterson locks a wheel on the March approaching
Druids Bend, Brands Hatch 1972.

THE veteran of France's rise to motor racing prominence in the 1960s, Jean-Pierre was a worker rather than an artist, many of his drives for Matra the product of a raw nationalistic fervour. Throughout 1968 and '69 he was content to remain in Jackie Stewart's shadow within the Matra squad, but took over as number one for the French team in 1970, using their own V12 engines. His greatest moment for Matra came at Clermont Ferrand that summer when it looked as though he had the French Grand Prix in the bag until the engine blew most of its oil away. In 1972 he drove for BRM and finally bagged his only Grand Prix win in torrential rain at Monaco, beating Jacky Ickx – acknowledged as the greatest wet-weather driver of his era – in a straight fight. It was proof that every driver has at least one great race within him. He never scaled such heights again, but kept racing saloon cars competitively for more than a decade after his F1 career came to an end. More than anything, JPB was a straightforward enthusiast.

EXTROVERT, charming and blessed with dazzling good looks, François Cevert was put on earth to be a racing driver. After enjoying considerable success in both F2 and F3, he was recruited to Formula 1 by Ken Tyrrell to partner Jackie Stewart early in 1970.

The bright-eyed young Frenchman proved a willing disciple of Stewart. By the summer of 1971 he was good enough to take second place behind JYS in the French Grand Prix and, with only a little luck, picked up a momentous victory at Watkins Glen later that year. Reckoned by some to be good enough to land a top drive elsewhere, Cevert remained an integral part of the Tyrrell family through 1972 and into '73. It was Ken's plan that François would inherit Stewart's position as number one driver when JYS retired.

Sadly, that transition never happened. Battling with Ronnie Peterson for a front row starting position at the Glen, Cevert was killed in a violent accident, and France had to wait for more than a decade before acclaiming its first World Champion.

SLOTTING almost perfectly into this section, Emerson's Grand Prix career began in 1970 highlighted by spectacular success. He won his fourth Grand Prix, the US race at Watkins Glen, to give Team Lotus a timely tonic following the tragic death of Jochen Rindt in practice at Monza. A decade later, it petered out almost unnoticed, driving for his own financially strapped team, his halcyon days all but forgotten.

Between those two divergent poles, Emerson Fittipaldi scaled terrific heights of success and plumbed depths of disappointment. An intuitive natural driver with great inborn skill and an analytical mind, he forged such a close bond with Colin Chapman that many were tempted to draw analogies with Jim Clark. It was Emerson who fully exploited the brilliant Lotus 72 to become the sport's youngest-ever World Champion – at the age of 23 in 1972 – but the lure of a lucrative Marlboro McLaren contract took him away from Lotus at the end of the following year, his morale slightly dented by the speed of his newly recruited team-mate Ronnie Peterson.

At McLaren he honed his driving style to perfection, handling the M23 with such consummate precision that it truly looked as though it was running on rails. He became World Champion again in 1974 and was runner-up to the Ferrari-mounted Niki Lauda the following year. But Emerson had always harboured ambitions of forming his own team and, in partnership with his older brother Wilson, shook the Grand Prix world by quitting McLaren for their newly established Copersucar outfit at the start of 1976. It was a mistake.

A succession of designers and years of dogged trying failed to mould the Fittipaldi brothers' enterprise into anything approaching a front-running outfit. But there was one more day of F1 glory to come Emerson's way. In 1978, in front of his home crowd at Rio de Janeiro, he brought the Copersucar home a storming second to Reutemann's Ferrari. Sadly, the flame of Fittipaldi's unquestionable talent was never rekindled again at the wheel of a Grand Prix car. Looking back, Emerson's great gift was squandered on an emotional spur-of-the-moment decision in the autumn of 1975. He never quite achieved the status that his early exploits suggested he would, but the potential for greatness was there. He can still be seen racing competitively to this day on the US Indy Car circuit.

Emerson Fittipaldi switched from Lotus to McLaren for
1974 and claimed his second World Championship.

TO some he was the classic all-American hero. Others simply looked on him as a rich kid got lucky. By the time Peter Revson hit his first winning streak in Formula 1 he was over 30, having first sampled F1 with a private Lotus-BRM in the early 1960s.

'Revvie' was determined, aggressive on his day and quite a stylist. He signed up with McLaren at the start of 1972 but it was not until he was in the cockpit of the splendid M23 for the '73 season that he had a car to unlock the door to Formula 1 success. He judged things superbly at Silverstone in the British GP, running the gauntlet of a rain shower to beat Peterson, Hulme and Hunt past the flag by a few seconds. Later that season he added the confused Canadian GP to his victory tally. But he fell out with the team's management and quit to join the fledgling Shadow outfit for 1974.

A banal accident while testing at Kyalami snatched away the handsome American just as he was establishing himself as a serious front-runner. I always thought he had a lot more to give.

RELAXED, easygoing and good natured, Peter Gethin seemed to lack that ruthless edge which marks out a World Champion from the average F1 driver. Having served an apprenticeship in the fledgling Formula 5000, Peter was taken under the McLaren team's wing and got his full-time break when Bruce McLaren was killed in the summer of 1970. He seemed little more than a good, solid midfield performer and produced no results of consequence before moving to BRM in the middle of 1971. He wrote his name into the pages of motor racing history when he risked everything on an audacious dive down the inside of his rivals going into Parabolica on the last corner of the Italian Grand Prix at Monza, out-dragging Ronnie Peterson to the line to win by one-hundredth of a second. Heroic wasn't the word for it, but 'Geth' was destined never to win in F1 again. A chirpy, popular character, he survived to retire from the cockpit and still remains on the fringes of the sport to this day.

The Seventies

JACKIE started the decade in a whirlwind of attention after winning his first championship at Monza with the Tyrrell Matra at the end of 1969. What followed next almost destroyed his self-confidence. Tyrrell had to become a March customer while the team's own car was secretly being completed and it turned out to be a ponderous truck by comparison with the agile Matra. Jackie almost worried himself to a standstill until the new Tyrrell appeared, allowing him to reassert his championship form in the last few races of the 1970 season.

But although Stewart cantered to the 1971 title, he lived a hectic business life in the fast lane and, alongside his motor racing, he was just taking too much out of himself. In 1972 he developed mononucleosis and a duodenal ulcer. Six weeks of enforced inactivity followed, during which his championship title slipped away yet again. In 1973 he won his third title and quit the cockpit at the end of the year, having made the decision to do so early in the season and kept it a secret for several months.

As a driver, Jackie honed the fine edge of his talent during the second phase of his career, but at the same time emerged as a more pragmatic performer. He minimised the risks in ruthlessly dispassionate fashion, never over-driving emotionally when the odds were stacked overwhelmingly against him. But when everything clicked, Jackie Stewart could still display a rare brilliance right through to the closing months of his career. He will always be remembered as the great star who drained all emotion from his driving, something which failed to find favour with the traditionalists. Perhaps that's one of the reasons he is still around for us to enjoy his endearing brand of cockiness to this day.

Stewart's Tyrrell heads a young Niki Lauda in the March
during the rain-lashed 1972 Monaco Grand Prix.

The Seventies

I first watched Niki Lauda in the European Formula 2 Trophy series in 1971 where this buck-toothed young Austrian's promise, skill and intelligence belied his inexperience. He moved into F1 on a 'rent-a-drive' basis the following year with March and it proved a humiliating experience which almost finished him once and for all. Once Niki had swollen the March bank balance he was left to sink or swim . . .

Ultimately, though, it was his pragmatic approach to the business side of motor racing which finally put him on the road to success. The way in which he coaxed and cajoled himself into the BRM team in 1973 gave us a foretaste of the razor-sharp commercial mind which would eventually help him become a millionaire from his chosen sport. Finally, he got the big break in '74 when he joined Ferrari, from which point he never looked back.

Shrewd, rational, methodical and able to make unemotional decisions, Niki Lauda quickly developed into the thinking man's Grand Prix driver of the 1970s. His rise to prominence was inextricably entwined with the Ferrari renaissance in the middle of the decade and, after a season's apprenticeship in 1974, he cantered to the championship the following year at the wheel of the splendid 312 *trasversale*. Then, in the summer of 1976, came his crash at the Nürburgring. He was badly burned about the head, but the damage to his lungs caused by scorching fumes did the most serious short-term damage. For a couple of days he hung precariously between life and death, but proceeded to make such a storming recovery that he was racing again in less than two months.

He failed to save his championship title from James Hunt's onslaught but bounced back in 1977, not only defeating his rivals to regain his title but also snubbing his nose at the 'Maranello mafia' who reckoned he was finished. At the end of the year he raised two fingers to Ferrari, leaving to join Brabham before retiring abruptly midway through practice for the 1979 Canadian Grand Prix. It seemed as though we had lost this remarkable personality for good to the world of aviation, but he was back in the cockpit just over two years later. As well as displaying total honesty, accurate self-appraisal and remarkable self-discipline, Niki Lauda was, on his day, also as quick as anybody on the track.

Niki Lauda rounds the Karussel on his way to third place
in the 1975 German Grand Prix at the Nürburgring.

WHAT many people failed to understand about Clay Regazzoni was his *passion* for racing. 'You must believe that, for me, winning is not as important as *being there*, being part of the scene,' he used to say. After gaining early celebrity status as a Ferrari team member, he switched to BRM for an unsuccessful season in 1973 before being welcomed back into the Maranello fold again for 1974. He was woefully inconsistent, taken over his career as a whole, but when he clicked he had the potential to win. But when he was having a bad day, half the grid knew about it . . .

Kicked out of Ferrari at the end of 1976, his career path took him via Ensign and Shadow to Williams. In 1979 he won Frank's first-ever F1 success – at Silverstone – but was dropped in favour of Reutemann at the end of the year. Partly paralysed after an accident for which he was blameless at Long Beach in 1980, Clay was henceforth relegated to the sidelines. A passionate, emotive and erratic racer, the sport could do with more people like the roughish, moustachioed Swiss.

HE was a perfectionist above all else. Enigmatic, serious and committed, Carlos Reutemann's personality was a baffling tangle of contradictions for much of his career. One day his brilliance would shine like a beacon and you were convinced he was the best driver of his era. The next weekend he would put in a pathetic performance, in no way worthy of his acknowledged status. He never managed to string together a successful title onslaught, but he was definitely serious championship material.

His successful formative years in F1 were spent with the Brabham team, but when Bernie Ecclestone switched to Alfa power, Carlos moved on to Ferrari where 1977 team-mate Lauda and Andretti in 1978 both threw the title beyond his reach.

In 1979 he switched to Lotus, but, again, it was the wrong decision. He raced on into the 1980s before giving it all up. Today he admits he retired too soon. A civilised and charming man, Carlos Reutemann basically failed to do justice to his own superb talent. But who can explain precisely why?

FOR much of his career, James seemed to treat his motor racing as a bit of a 'wizard wheeze' with plenty of birds and off-track boozing to make the party swing. But that was only a superficial view of the man's incredibly inconsistent form. There were days when he drove *brilliantly* – there's no other word for it – but one always had the feeling, rightly it turned out, that Formula 1 wasn't the be-all and end-all for the Wellington-educated racer.

James won his Grand Prix spurs with the Hesketh team where Bubbles Horsley should be given credit for bringing the best out of James, helping him immeasurably to mature as a driver. His victory in the '75 Dutch Grand Prix, where he beat Lauda's Ferrari in a straight fight, underlined the fact that there was more to Hunt than had met the eye during his chaotic early years in F3. The McLaren team was the beneficiary of his new-found maturity, as they drafted James into their ranks after Fittipaldi's defection to his family team. As history records, Hunt won the '76 title, but that stark fact conceals some terrific races. Nürburgring, Zandvoort, Mosport Park and Watkins Glen all fell to James in sparkling style. In 1977 he won several more Grand Prix victories, but McLaren was slow to climb aboard the ground-effect bandwagon and, faced with the prospect of assuming the role of also-ran, James's performances became rather patchy and unpredictable.

By the end of 1978 he was finished with McLaren and moved to join Walter Wolf's *équipe*. But he retired after a handful of races, unhappy about the way in which the latest breed of ground-effect cars were evolving with their rock hard suspension systems. A driver whose fans loved him dearly and detractors disliked him vehemently, James was always very much his own man. Even if you judged him lucky to win his sole World Championship title, he drove some fine individual races and remained resolutely and defiantly independent to the day he quit the sport.

Made in Japan . . . James Hunt's measured drive in
atrocious conditions at the Mount Fuji circuit brought
him the 1976 championship.

AN ideal and devoted team-mate to Mario Andretti, Gunnar's tragically
brief career spanned only a couple of F1 seasons, but he left a sufficiently
strong impression at Team Lotus to be remembered as an unusually
talented rising star. He admired Mario enormously, had bags of raw enthusiasm
and was happy learning his F1 trade at a time when Lotus was dragging itself out
of a disappointing two-year run of poor equipment and missed opportunities.

In 1977, armed with the Lotus 78 'wing car', Gunnar drove a well-judged race in
atrocious conditions to win the soaking Belgian Grand Prix at Zolder. He was a
cheery soul with a gregarious nature, but his driving became patchy towards
the end of the '77 season and it began to look as though he was finding the whole
business physically taxing. What we did not know at the time was that he had the
early symptoms of cancer. He signed to drive for the Arrows team in 1978, but was
never well enough to race the car. He battled manfully against his illness throughout the summer and finally died in the autumn. It was a bitter loss.

B ERNIE Ecclestone isn't exactly renowned for his love of racing drivers. Catch him in the right mood and he will confess that in the last thirty years there have been perhaps four he has really had a lot of time for. One of them was Carlos Pace. In fact, Bernie once said, 'if Carlos had lived, then I wouldn't have needed Niki Lauda.' That stands as the most eloquent testimony to the debonair Brazilian, whose sole Grand Prix victory came in front of his home crowd at Interlagos in 1975. Armed with Bernie's compact Brabham BT44B, 'Moco' Pace beat fellow Paulistano Emerson Fittipaldi's McLaren in a straight fight. The scenes of delight that followed made Ferrari victory celebrations at Monza seem like a tea party on the vicarage lawn.

An obviously gifted rising star, Pace served his F1 apprenticeship with Williams and Surtees before joining Brabham midway through 1974. When the team switched to Alfa power he persevered doggedly with the project, in contrast to team-mate Reutemann who just gave up all hope. The whole project was just coming right when Pace died in a private plane crash near São Paulo shortly after the 1977 South African Grand Prix.

AN incurable romantic, I always thought Jochen arrived in F1 about 20 years after the era which would have best suited him. Sensitive, intelligent and caring, this pleasant German was a fine racing driver, but allowed himself to be psychologically undermined by unsympathetic team managers and team-mates. He was never quite a number one, but emerged as one of the best number twos in the game, particularly at McLaren before he was worn down by a combination of James Hunt and Teddy Mayer, with neither of whom he could really hit it off. After his halcyon days at McLaren – during which he won the tragic, shortened 1975 Spanish race at Barcelona – he joined ATS and Arrows. The saddest moment came when he was involved in Gilles Villeneuve's fatal practice accident at Zolder in 1982. Disillusioned and saddened, he quit F1 at the end of the year. He is still regarded with enormous affection by those who were lucky enough to know him.

THIS dogged Italian driver was a rough old number, pushed on throughout his career by an obsessive and unquenchable enthusiasm for driving way over his head. But he got so much pure pleasure from his sport – seemingly even when crashing – that he became one of the most popular personalities in the pit lane. To be frank, Vittorio made Andrea de Cesaris look cool and composed. But he was quick on his day, planting his March on pole position for the 1975 Swedish Grand Prix, and when he won the rain-reduced, half-distance Austrian Grand Prix he crossed the line punching the air so enthusiastically that he promptly lost control and spun into the guard rail just beyond the finishing line. In some ways he was a one-man disaster area but the crowd loved him and F1 insiders were always kept entertained by the innocent way in which he tried to explain away his errors. Despite being hurt in the multiple shunt which cost Ronnie Peterson his life at Monza in 1978, Vittorio happily recovered to retire from the sport in one piece. A thoroughly good bloke.

A man with star quality stamped through his personality like a stick of Brighton rock. Charismatic, civilised and every inch a racing driver, Mario Andretti's victory in the 1978 World Championship was but one facet of a career which embodied every imaginable category of the sport.

He kicked off his F1 successes with victory for Ferrari in the 1971 South African Grand Prix, but it was not until 1976 that he really gave F1 his undivided attention, helping Colin Chapman haul Lotus back from the edge of technical oblivion. Then came the team's pioneering work at the start of the ground-effect era and two magnificent seasons, 1977 and '78. To see him at work in the majestic Lotus 79 was a rare glimpse of man and machine in total harmony. Car and driver almost talked to each other, forging a technical bond which paid off superbly. Chapman likened their special relationship to that which he had enjoyed with Jim Clark.

Mario was a natural talent, his gift spiced by a streak of impetuosity which perhaps reflected his Italian origins. Occasionally he would become overexcited in the first-lap scramble and make a fundamental error which would cost him the race. But the credits overwhelmingly outweighed the debits. It was a shame to watch him struggling with sub-standard equipment as Lotus's technical advantage evaporated into 1979 and '80.

Eventually, he spent his final F1 season with Alfa Romeo, but it amounted to a complete waste of time. By then over 40, he returned to concentrate his efforts on Indy Car racing, but could never quite leave F1 alone. In 1982 he was offered a 'guest' appearance in a Ferrari 126 turbo at Monza. It was a truly emotional moment, like some sort of symbolic homecoming of a long-exiled hero. He planted it on pole position to round off a Grand Prix career which still glitters brightly in the mind's eye almost two decades after his title success. Sheer class sums it all up . . .

Mario Andretti enjoyed mixed fortunes during his two seasons at Ferrari. He is pictured leading Pedro Rodriguez in the 1971 Spanish Grand Prix.

T HE good-looking Swede seemed set for stardom from the moment he first climbed into an F1 cockpit. Three barren seasons with the March team left him hungry for success, so when he joined Team Lotus to handle the brilliant type 72 as Emerson Fittipaldi's team-mate in 1973, the world held its breath . . .

Nobody was disappointed. His thrilling car control had Chapman's baby dancing on the outer limits of adhesion round every track on which it raced. But the World Championship eluded him. He stayed with Lotus for the next two years, but as the team lost its technical edge, his extrovert driving style became progressively more frantic as prospects of further victories evaporated. His moves to March (1976) and Tyrrell (1977) were unproductive, but an opportunity to rebuild his reputation came in 1978 when he rejoined Lotus – as number two to Mario Andretti. It was a dignified decision made by an honourable man. When he died from injuries sustained in a startline pile-up at Monza the F1 world was pole-axed. Nobody ever had a bad word to say against Ronnie, for as well as being a terrific racer he was quite simply a lovely guy.

PATRICK Depailler was the 'little boy lost' amongst the generation of French new-boys led by François Cevert in the early 1970s. Genial, slightly nervous, but totally embroiled in the business of motor racing, this slightly built Frenchman seemed destined to be cast in the role of supporting star for much of his career. But a win at Monaco in 1978 boosted his reputation and, when Guy Ligier expanded his operation to run a second car in 1979, Patrick was picked to partner Jacques Laffite. He won the Spanish Grand Prix, but then injured himself badly by crashing a hang glider and was invalided out for the rest of the year. Bloody-minded tenacity dragged him back to the cockpit for 1980, only for Patrick to be killed testing his Alfa Romeo at Hockenheim. It was a tragic waste.

ARLY in his career they called him 'Baby Bear' because he was schooled by Denny 'The Bear' Hulme during his first few races with McLaren. Later he was nicknamed 'Fletcher' after the over-ambitious baby seagull in the book *Jonathan Livingstone Seagull* who was always trying to fly before he was ready to, inevitably crashing into the pit face as a result. He exploded onto the European scene in 1971, driving Formula Ford, and by the end of the following season was making his F1 debut at the wheel of a McLaren at Watkins Glen. By the summer of '73 he could be seen leading the French Grand Prix at Paul Ricard – and destroying half the pack a few weeks later as he triggered a multi-car pile-up which brought the British Grand Prix to a premature halt!

Most people thought Jody would never live to a ripe old age. Despite his obvious lack of experience, the cocky South African set such a fearsome pace in those early days that most watched his progress with their hands partially covering their eyes, waiting for The Big Shunt. Thankfully, it never happened and Jody settled down in 1974 to drive three seasons with Ken Tyrrell. He won a handful of Grands Prix, but by the end of '76 many people believed he had lost his edge. He proved them wrong in 1977, winning three races for the revitalised Walter Wolf team and coming within sniffing distance of the championship.

In 1979 he moved to Ferrari. Most touchline observers thought this was the end. That stroppy South African and all those hysterical Italians – a recipe for disaster. Not so! 'Fletch' got on famously at Maranello and won the World Championship, despite having Gilles Villeneuve as his team-mate. At the end of the following year he retired, barely 30 years old. He matured into a relaxed, popular campaigner with an appealing, slightly world-weary sense of humour. And in the cockpit, he had it all nicely worked out, wiping away his early impulsiveness and replacing it with a controlled aggression that worked well for him.

Jody Scheckter won in Sweden and collected points consistently in 1976 with the amazing six-wheeled Tyrrell. Here he heads for third place in the Belgian Grand Prix.

INTROSPECTIVE and modest, Jean-Pierre Jabouille's fleeting taste of Grand Prix success came hand-in-hand with the rise of Renault as a Formula 1 force. A methodical test driver blessed with a disarmingly easy temperament, he helped bring the French team's turbo efforts to fruition over two years of painstaking development. The reward for all this toil was victory in the French Grand Prix at Dijon in 1979, followed up by a disciplined and well-judged win, by a second or so, from Alan Jones's Williams at the Österreichring the following summer. That latter race demonstrated Jabouille's true calibre. Armed with a much faster car, he did the minimum necessary to keep Jones off the victory rostrum. No drama, no heroics, just the sensible use of the machinery beneath him.

Signed by Ligier for 1981, he sustained serious leg injuries in his Renault at Montreal in his last-but-one race for the team. It knocked the stuffing out of him. Although he returned to the cockpit, he was never the same driver and retired after a handful of races.

IS sheer *joie de vivre* and zest for life has always been infectious. His driving reflected the competitiveness of his car. As Keke Rosberg, his team-mate for two years at Williams, explained, 'Give Jacques the best car and he'll run at the front. Give him the worst and he will be nowhere.' Jacques' driving style was smooth and crisp, with an artistic flow that made you think he could have developed into a great driver. But he was never serious enough for that. Life was for living and motor racing was part of that life. But only part of it. He had no hang-ups and, even when well over 40, occasionally looked a potential winner in his Ligier-Renault.

A great friend of Alain Prost, with whom he would use almost any excuse to nip off early after practice in order to play golf, Jacques retains a keen and unquenchable sense of humour which endured through a painful recovery from the accident which ended his career at Brands Hatch in 1986. At Dallas in 1984 the race morning warm-up took place at 7.30 a.m. Jacques arrived at the circuit wearing only his pyjamas. That said it all about the guy . . .

IF you'd watched Tony Brise shaking his fist as he tried to lap his Embassy Hill team-mate Alan Jones in the rain-soaked 1975 Dutch Grand Prix, you might have come to the conclusion that the Australian wasn't much cop. But, as with so many self-made stars, Alan only needed some half-decent equipment under him to make his mark. Out in the wilderness with no apparent future, he got his big chance with Shadow after Tom Pryce was killed at the start of 1977, and picked up a lucky win in that summer's Austrian Grand Prix. Clearly, he was performing better than the Shadow and his bulldog tenacity earned him a place in the revitalised Williams team for 1978.

At first progress was steady rather than spectacular but when Patrick Head's world-beating ground-effect Williams FW07 was introduced the following season, Alan squeezed every last ounce of potential out of it. By the time the new car was fully reliable, the World Championship was already a distant prospect but four wins in the last six races gave every indication of the combination's potential. The Didcot team set the pace from the outset in 1980 and Alan overcame a spirited challenge from Nelson Piquet to take the title with five more wins. A true child of the ground-effect era, Jones displayed tremendous consistency, iron nerve and an unremitting will to win. He was a fighter more than an artist, but a ferociously determined one, whose contribution to the emergence of the Williams team as a major force in Grand Prix racing was considerable.

Alan elected to retire at the end of the 1981 season, signing off in brilliant style with an unchallenged victory in the Las Vegas Grand Prix. But the Australian didn't leave it at that. After a year racing a Porsche sports car in Australia, Jonesey yearned for wider racing horizons. He dabbled with an F1 comeback with Arrows in 1983 and, although that came to nothing, he returned to Grand Prix racing full time with the Carl Haas-operated Beatrice Lola team late in 1985. The cars were not fully competitive, however, and the sharp edge of Jones's racing appetite seemed to have been blunted. He soldiered on through 1986 before returning to Australia once more. Sadly it had been a somewhat inconsequential encore to a valiant F1 career.

Ending on a high note. Alan Jones leads the pack into the
first corner of the 1981 Las Vegas Grand Prix to record a
final victory in his last race for Williams before
retirement. His subsequent reappearances failed to meet
with the same success.

T HIS popular Ulsterman always seemed to make life more complicated for himself than it needed to be. His was a terrific natural talent which, like Reutemann's, never really came to full flower, though for different reasons. John was perpetually trying to rationalise and over-analyse his own personal race performances and was such a perfectionist that he tended to fiddle round with chassis settings chasing some elusive compromise, rather than going out and hurling the car about by the scruff of its neck.

Paradoxically, when John really got the wind up his tail he was a hard man to beat. His blend of skill and speed was probably at its peak in 1977 and '78 whilst driving the Brabham-Alfas, cars which habitually let him down. The French Grand Prix in '77 was a classic example, his BT45B hiccupping low on fuel two corners from home. He should have won that race – but then those six words encapsulate the story of John's F1 life.

JEAN-PIERRE JARIER:
Moody, inconsistent, but very quick on his day.

MARK DONOHUE:
Experienced, methodical and restrained. His death was
due to causes unfairly outside his control.

TONY BRISE:
So much more to offer.

ROGER WILLIAMSON:
Rugged rising star killed before his prime.

TOM PRYCE *(right)*: One of Britain's lost F1 generation.

HANS STUCK *(below)*: Magnificent car control, but short on single-mindedness. The talent was there, but not the commitment.

MIKE HAILWOOD *(below)*: A sunny and uninhibited character whose innate brilliance never got the chance to shine through on four wheels.

ROLF STOMMELEN *(bottom)*: His early promise was never quite sustained.

Niki Lauda's dreadful accident in the 1976 German
Grand Prix at the Nürburgring opened the door for
James Hunt, who took his opportunity brilliantly to
win the World Championship by a single point.
Six victories were recorded with the McLaren
M23, including the Dutch Grand Prix *(above)*.

A familiar sight in 1978 – Lotus team-mates Mario
Andretti and Ronnie Peterson head the field. For
Mario the championship was the reward for his efforts
in leading the Hethel team out of the doldrums. The
brilliant and much loved Peterson was to die following
an accident at the start of the Italian Grand Prix, the
very race at which Mario clinched the title.

The 1980 World Champion, Alan Jones, forged a formidable alliance with team owner Frank Williams and designer Patrick Head. Their success proved there was still room at the top for those with talent and dedication.

Jody Scheckter's ability marked him as a potential champion as early as 1973. This promise was finally fulfilled in 1979 after a move to Ferrari. *Below:* The South African is shadowed by team-mate Gilles Villeneuve on his way to victory in the Monaco Grand Prix of that year.

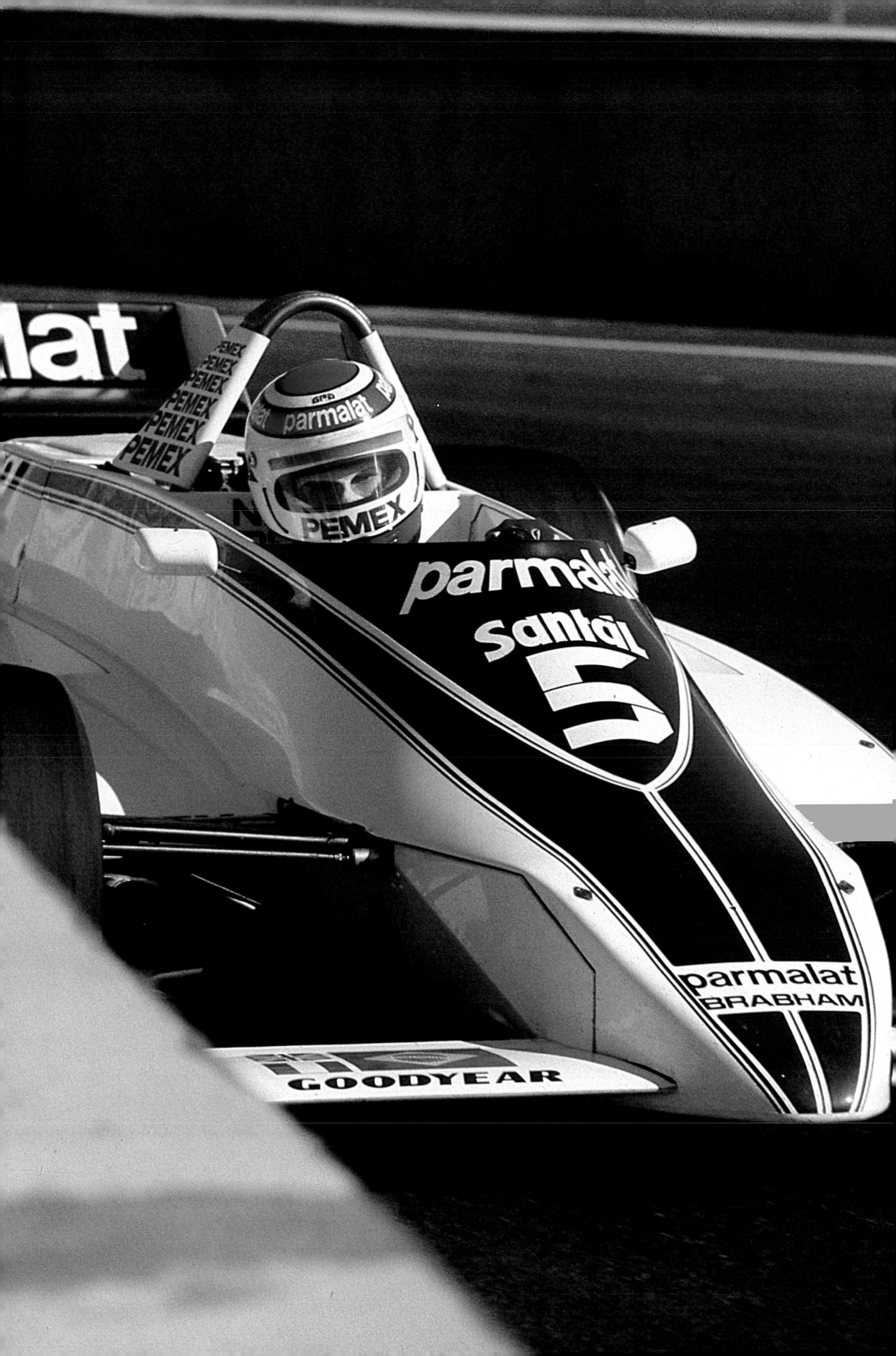

parmalat
santal
5
parmalat
BRABHAM
GOODYEAR
PEMEX
PEMEX

Nelson Piquet *(left)* enjoyed a tremendous rapport with Brabham designer Gordon Murray and their partnership yielded two world titles in 1981 and 1983.

Keke Rosberg struggled to qualify the Fittipaldi in 1981, but a move to Williams saw him crowned World Champion the following season.

Niki Lauda pipped Alain Prost to the 1984 title by just half a point. The McLaren pair won 12 of the 16 races between them; Lauda's win at the Österreichring *(above)* was the only occasion on which he was to win his home Grand Prix.

After seven Grand Prix wins in 1984 and
still no World Championship, Alain Prost made
no mistake the following year. His win at Monaco
(left) was just another step on the way to
championships in 1985 and 1986.

The Williams-Hondas set the pace in 1986 but the
intense rivalry between new recruit Nelson Piquet
and team-mate Nigel Mansell allowed Alain Prost to
snatch the title at the last round. Piquet learned his
lesson, however, easing his way to the 1987 World
Championship with a blend of speed and consistency.
He is pictured leading the pack into the first corner in
Brazil, ahead of Ayrton Senna's Lotus and
Alessandro Nannini's Benetton.

The combination of Honda turbo engines, McLaren's
peerless standards of organisation, the proven
excellence of Alain Prost and the volatile genius of
Ayrton Senna rewrote the Grand Prix history books in
1988. Between them the pair won all but one of the
season's 16 races, the Brazilian *(below)* taking the
title with a record-breaking eight victories.

It was almost inevitable that the partnership between
Alain Prost and Ayrton Senna, the two outstanding
drivers of their generation and two of the all-time
greats, would dissolve amid bitterness and
recrimination. Prost *(above right)* grabbed the 1989
World Championship after a controversial collision in
Japan but Senna *(right)* was generally faster and
scored two wins more than the Frenchman.

Ayrton Senna *(below)* remained with McLaren in 1990 while Alain Prost *(bottom)* switched to Ferrari. The powerful Honda V10 helped Senna to six victories but Prost's legendary ability as a test driver was seen once more as he honed the Italian car into a formidable contender. The title was finally settled in the Brazilian's favour by a clash with his rival at the start of the Japanese Grand Prix that, in many eyes, tarnished the crown he had gained.

The McLaren-Honda alliance secured its fourth drivers' championship in succession in 1991, Ayrton Senna holding off a strong challenge from Nigel Mansell's Williams to claim his third title. The Brazilian is seen *(right)* leading the field out to practise at Spa, where he went on to win.

After ten seasons in Formula 1, Nigel Mansell
returned to Williams in 1991 in a bid to win the World
Championship that had been snatched from his grasp
so cruelly five years earlier. Mechanical failures
frustrated his efforts but the following season he
crushed all opposition in majestic style: his win in the
German Grand Prix at Hockenheim *(left)* was his
eighth in the first ten races.

Ayrton Senna's victory in the 1993 Grand Prix of
Europe *(top)* at Donington Park confirmed that there
are circumstances in which the gifts of the man in the
cockpit can still compensate for the deficiencies of his
car, but the year belonged to Alain Prost *(above)*, who
cruised to the title at the wheel of a Williams-Renault
enjoying a significant power advantage.

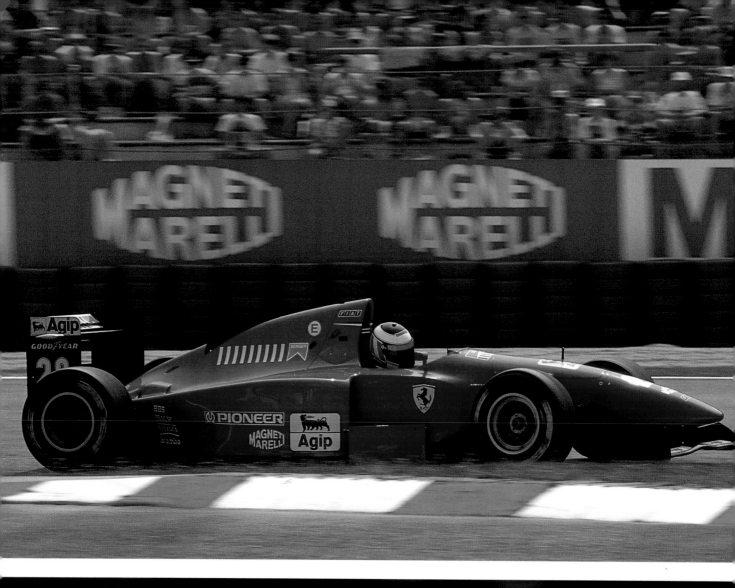

Gerhard Berger scored his first win as long ago as
1986 but has yet to mount a serious championship
challenge. The likeable Austrian's popular victory in
the 1994 German Grand Prix *(left)* was a timely
reminder of his true class.

In only his second full season of Grand Prix racing
Damon Hill *(below left)* was thrust into the role of
Williams team leader following the death of Ayrton
Senna. He responded magnificently, taking the World
Championship battle to the final race of the season.

Nigel Mansell returned from his exile in Indy Car
racing to compete in four races for Williams in 1994.
He started the last of them, the Australian Grand
Prix in Adelaide *(above)*, from pole position and went
on to score the 31st victory of his distinguished career.

The 1994 season saw the emergence of Michael
Schumacher *(overleaf)* as Grand Prix racing's latest
superstar. He took the championship with eight
victories from 14 starts in the Benetton-Ford but
controversy haunted the unfortunate German
every step of the way.

THE EIGHTIES

By Maurice Hamilton

Fierce rivals: Nigel Mansell's Williams-Honda
leads Ayrton Senna's Lotus-Renault in
the 1986 French Grand Prix.

TALKING to him, you would never have known this was the most naturally gifted driver of his day. Watch him on the track and there would be no doubt.

Gilles Villeneuve had spine-tingling flair. It was an asset which he exploited to the full, largely because he enjoyed the sensation of sliding a racing car under power. That raw enthusiasm reached the spectators, giving the feeling this was not merely work; it was fun. But that should not suggest that Villeneuve was foolhardy. In his own way, he was totally dedicated to winning.

There were no big egos when Gilles was around. Devoid of pretension, Villeneuve preferred to stay with his wife and children in a camper, which he would park in the paddock. The mechanics at Ferrari, for whom he drove almost exclusively in Formula 1, adored him for it.

He died at Zolder in May 1982, giving his all in a Ferrari. Some said that he was reckless, that he had it coming. Others, with a deeper appreciation of his genius, felt no comment was necessary. Gilles Villeneuve's input to motor racing during an all too brief period had said it all.

ERE was the man who had everything: boyish good looks, a strong physique, style both on and off the track, and a works Ferrari drive to boot. All told, it gave him confidence . . . a great deal of confidence.

In August 1982, he was leading the championship by nine points. Nothing, it seemed, could stop him. Fastest in practice on the first day of the German Grand Prix, he went out the following morning in pouring rain. Fastest again. Then he crashed, the severe leg injuries ending his career right there, on the fast approach to the Hockenheim stadium.

The thing about Didier Pironi was that, had he succeeded in 1982, he could have won the championship again and again. His supreme talent and cleancut appearance guaranteed a place in the plans of any top-drawer team or sponsor. He was well-educated, soft-spoken and mild-mannered. Yet he barely acknowledged his mechanics while racing for Tyrrell, the team which brought him into Formula 1 in 1978. Underneath the acceptable façade was a ruthless determination to get his way.

Pironi later turned to power boat racing but lost his life during a race in the English Channel in 1987 – the final irony in a career which had promised so much.

NELSON Piquet's Grand Prix career began in a blaze of glory with Brabham, when he became World Champion twice; he later won a third world title, with Williams, but found his reputation under siege. By the time the Brazilian left F1, the enigma created ten years before had been badly compromised. The problem for Nelson was that his early years as a shooting star made his subsequent decline from a great height seem sadly dramatic. And it was no coincidence, perhaps, that Brabham should fail to win another race following Nelson's departure at the end of 1985.

The relationship between Piquet and Brabham amounted to a special kind of kinship, each working for the other and united by a love of the sport. Bernie Ecclestone's eye for a sharp deal saw him pick Piquet up for a song not long after the 26-year-old from Rio de Janeiro had made his first two F1 appearances with private entrants half-way through the 1978 season.

Piquet, very much one of the boys, quickly forged an affinity with the mechanics and Brabham's *avant garde* designer, Gordon Murray. Nelson's capacity for endless testing and conversations about motor racing sparked Murray's genius and the team's enthusiasm; together, they destroyed the opposition in 1981, and again two years later.

Piquet was crafty, but also lazy, and he was ill-equipped to cope with the hammering dealt out by Nigel Mansell when, in search of a decent salary for the first time, Piquet joined Williams-Honda in 1986 for two turbulent seasons. Mansell's storming technique swept aside the more subtle approach favoured by his team-mate and, between them, they allowed the 1986 title-chase to slip through their fingers. Piquet brought his tally of Grand Prix wins to 20 with three victories in 1987 as he claimed his third world crown but the ensuing mutual separation would favour Williams more than Piquet as Nelson joined Lotus, a once-great team at the beginning of a sad decline.

With his motivation flagging as he struggled with a poor car, Piquet saw out the decade absent from the limelight in every sense as he retreated as often as possible to Monte Carlo and his beloved boat. It seemed to be the end of a great career but there was to be one last hurrah. To the surprise of most observers he was invited to join Benetton in 1990 and silenced his detractors with two end-of-season wins, one fortunate, the other earned the hard way after a thrilling battle with Mansell. The following season brought a third victory but at the end of it he found that his services were no longer required by a team that had recently signed Michael Schumacher. Nelson decided to try his luck at Indianapolis but tragically suffered serious leg injuries in a practice crash that ended his front-line career.

Nelson Piquet joined Williams-Honda for 1986 with a
third World Championship in prospect, only to find
himself upstaged by team-mate Nigel Mansell.
The Brazilian leads Michele Alboreto at Monza
on his way to victory in the Italian Grand Prix.

The Eighties

THE artist, Jim Bamber, produced a cartoon in 1984 depicting Riccardo Patrese and his Alfa Romeo team-mate, Eddie Cheever. Bamber portrayed them in separate cages on wheels, trying to kick and claw at each other through the bars. It was not far from the truth. This was during Patrese's eighth season in Formula 1 and he was not much more than a figure of fun, a driver with great promise who had somehow failed to deliver. It was true that Patrese had already won two Grands Prix, but neither victory could be considered a classic in the sense that he thoroughly deserved the result. Patrese's huge natural ability had been squandered with Arrows, Brabham and Alfa Romeo. His Italian temperament seemed incapable of coping to the point where the frustration degenerated, both on and off the track, into squabbles with his equally volatile team-mate. It was only when he joined Williams at the end of 1987 that Riccardo's experience and speed began to find a more comfortable home. Despite a sometimes moody temperament, Patrese was essentially dignified and loyal, a private man who shunned the politics and the hype. More fitting results would come as his lengthy career reached its peak with the British team.

WHEN awarded the Renault drive which brought him into Formula 1 full time, René Arnoux cried. It was indicative of a man of emotion, most of which the Grand Prix world never fully understood, try as they might.

Arnoux was a strange mixture of earthy talent and agricultural habits. His casual attire may have reflected a nonchalant air as he trudged through the paddock but, once in the car, a fiery nature accounted for brilliant drives and belligerent behaviour, sometimes in the same afternoon.

Despite his provincial accent, the chic French F1 set had no complaints when he won four Grands Prix and took 14 pole positions for Renault. That natural car control was what attracted the attention of Enzo Ferrari. Moving to Maranello was, perhaps, René's biggest mistake. The Italian habit of deifying Ferrari drivers suited him too well. He left behind his wife and family and, it seemed, a good deal of sound judgement. There were three wins plus a brilliant second place earned purely on reflex at Dallas. But there were also inexplicable moments; inconsistent actions. His carefree character proved better suited to the more relaxed environment at Ligier, where he saw out the final years of his F1 career with little distinction.

THE gold bracelet, the cigarette palmed between thumb and forefinger, the Ray-Ban sunglasses and long hair. These were the Rosberg trademarks every bit as much as his flamboyant attitude on the track. And certainly more so than his entry in the record book.

The statistics show that Keijo 'Keke' Rosberg from Helsinki raced for nine years in Formula 1 and averaged 17 points per season (Alain Prost scored 59 on average). He struggled to finish each year among the top five point scorers although, in 1982, he did win the title. Even then, his championship year was tainted slightly by a single victory in a season which had been going the way of Didier Pironi until the accident which put the Frenchman out of racing for good.

But such mundane data is irrelevant when discussing one of the few characters to have brightened Grand Prix racing in the Eighties. Rosberg defied convention in every sense, not least with his cocky attitude out of the car and an apparent disdain for the driving textbooks when at the wheel. It was his urgent, unforgiving style which appealed to the spectators, a forceful method which said everything about his appetite for racing and winning.

In the summer of 1978, Rosberg raced 41 times in the space of 36 weekends. It was a relentless schedule which embraced Formula Atlantic racing in North America and his opening season of Formula 1 for the little-known Theodore team. Rosberg's name came unexpectedly to the fore when he won his first F1 race, a non-championship event held in teeming conditions at Silverstone. The entry may have been weak but Rosberg kept control while the big names ran into trouble.

His career continued to be a mixture of formulae and snatched opportunities – half-way through 1979, for example, when asked to replace James Hunt at Wolf after the former champion had suddenly retired. But his biggest break came in 1982 when Rosberg found himself leading the Williams team after Alan Jones had quit at the end of the previous season and the Argentinian driver, Carlos Reutemann, abandoned F1 at the outbreak of the Falklands War.

Within seven months, Rosberg had won the title and it mattered little how he had achieved it. His cheerful disregard for convention went down well with sponsors, who got their money's worth in the paddock and on the track. His final year, spent with McLaren in 1986, was disappointing by Keke's blistering standards but the lure of wheeling and dealing has kept him involved in a managerial capacity as he introduces his young protégés to a well-balanced but thoroughly professional approach to a sport he clearly enjoyed to the full.

The 1985 Australian race was to be Keke Rosberg's final
Grand Prix win for Williams. His move to McLaren
proved to be a major disappointment.

W HEN protesting drivers locked themselves in a Johannesburg hotel in 1982, Elio de Angelis soothed many a frayed nerve by playing classical music on a piano. In some ways, that musical talent seemed better suited to his gentle, polite manner than was the hurly-burly of Formula 1. Yet Elio had the handsome, Italian cut of a racing driver, and even if his hunger to succeed may not have been as sharp as that of some of his rivals, he used that same finger-tip flair to take his car to the limit.

Perhaps his best days were with Shadow in 1979. Agreed, money had got him that far but he had something to prove and used his inherent ability to work an uncompetitive car into places where it ought not to have been.

After that, Lotus and Brabham – and two Grand Prix wins. It is an inappropriate epitaph to a charming, highly skilled racing driver who felt that there was a little more to life than Formula 1. And that made his death during a test session at Paul Ricard in 1986 seem all the more unnecessary.

THE highlight of his career was a win at Imola, driving Ferrari number 27, the car which previously belonged to Gilles Villeneuve. When Gilles died, Tambay was chosen as his friend's replacement. It was, in Patrick's eyes, an honour and he did it justice by avenging Villeneuve's defeat at Imola the previous year. To any other driver, it would simply have been a very nice win. For Patrick Tambay, it was almost preordained, such was his sensitive nature.

That acute awareness, of course, got him in the end. There is no room for nice guys in Formula 1 and Tambay was, unquestionably, a gentleman. French by birth, a period in the United States gave him a delightful accent and a fluency in English. A former ski champion, Patrick looked every inch a Grand Prix driver. He played it too, particularly when Ferrari salvaged a career which appeared to be snared by his self-effacing manner.

There were low periods with McLaren and Ligier. But, when on top form, believing fully in himself and a first-rate car, Tambay was unbeatable. Unfortunately for motor racing, those days were all too rare.

The Eighties

THE story about the car wash has been told many times, but it bears repeating. Trophies, by and large, were meaningless to Niki Lauda and he reached an agreement with his local garage. They could display the silverware in their window in return for free car washes. Business is business and it was always so from the moment Niki Lauda arranged a £30,000 loan to buy his way into Formula 1.

Lauda's cold, commercial approach seemed to extend to his driving. There was no tingling excitement about it; no opposite lock. There was a job to be done and the motivation was doing it better than anyone else. Power slides and tyre smoke were all very well – but they were a waste of time and effort, a diversion from the realisation of the perfect lap in practice and nine points at the end of the weekend's work. Earn enough points and you win the championship. You can keep the trophies.

By the summer of 1979, the garage was decked out with the trappings of two World Championships and 17 wins. What next? The realisation that there was little else to achieve dawned about 11.0 on the morning of 28 September during practice for the Canadian Grand Prix. By 11.30, Niki Lauda, retired racing driver, was on his way to the airport to pursue the challenge of expanding his commercial airline, LaudaAir.

At 30, he had been, in his words, to hell and back. A terrible accident at the Nürburgring in 1976 had almost killed him. The second championship less than a year later was a startling display of mind over matter. It was almost as if the need to recover had itself provided the necessary stimulant. It was the same when he revitalised the shambling Ferrari team in 1974. It was the same when he returned to watch a Formula 1 race in 1981.

Now we had ground-effect cars which called for physical fitness and a totally different driving technique. This was new to Lauda and his curiosity was primed. Was it possible to come back and drive one of these cars? Could he win a race again? He was hooked. Like a man flirting with a jilted lover merely to keep her hopes alive and boost his ego, Lauda returned to prove he could assert his will over these infinitely more difficult cars.

It *was* different but that was precisely why he relished the challenge; why further wins were almost a foregone conclusion. When he clinched the championship with McLaren for a third time at Estoril in 1984, that toothy grin said as much as the scarred face which told of a remarkable man who had seen and done it all.

Lauda retired for good and returned his full attention to an airline which was poised to explore the world market. That logical and forthright business manner is also employed in his role as adviser to Ferrari. The fact is that motor racing is literally seared into his subconscious.

Comebacks are usually a bad idea, but Niki Lauda
returned to claim a third championship. His McLaren
wins the 1984 British Grand Prix at Brands Hatch.

The Eighties

ALAIN Prost never quite received the credit he deserved, a record 51 Grand Prix wins and four world titles somehow being unfairly tainted by controversy. Prost was inclined to say what he thought but the effect of his softly articulated complaints was the easy inheritance of a reputation as a whinger. And, when he voiced his dislike of racing on a soaking track, he was branded a wimp not fit to be included with the truly great racing drivers.

Alain Prost is worthy of discussion in the same breath as Fangio, Moss and Clark. It is just unfortunate that he had to race head-to-head with Ayrton Senna. Had either driver been free to dominate his era without the threat posed by the other, acrimony would have been avoided and his statistical record would have reached stratospheric proportions. As it is, Prost's tally, ten more than Senna's, is likely to stand for some time.

Prost opened his account in 1981, the year he joined Renault after an impressive debut season with McLaren. When Prost was made the scapegoat for Renault's third successive failure to win the championship, he rushed into the arms of the revamped McLaren team and finished runner-up to Niki Lauda in the 1984 title race before securing his first championship the following year.

Prost's trademark was persistent application of his technical excellence and shrewd tactical brain, allied to a deceptively smooth driving style. A firm believer in making the car do all the work, Alain appeared to glide to the title when he took advantage of the squabbling between the Williams drivers in 1986. He would get a taste of in-house rivalry himself when Senna joined McLaren in 1988 and began to erode Prost's confidence.

The McLaren-Honda superteam achieved total domination in 1988, winning all but one of the season's races, but the competition between its two star drivers was intense. Although Prost scored more points it was Senna who deservedly took the title but the following season the relationship between the pair, never better than polite, steadily deteriorated. It was clearly impossible for them to remain in the same team any longer and in September Prost announced that he would be joining Ferrari in 1990. Alain's six-year stay at Woking was to end amid bitter recriminations when, tiring of his team-mate's aggression, he clumsily contributed to Senna's removal from the penultimate race in an incident that gave the Frenchman his third World Championship.

Further controversy lay ahead.

Alain Prost clocked up victories with apparent ease; his 27th, in the 1987 Belgian Grand Prix, equalled Jackie Stewart's long-standing record.

The Eighties

HIS first Grand Prix win – Portugal, 1985 – was utterly brilliant. In some ways it was a foretaste of what was to come, a display in atrocious conditions of skill, commitment, courage and startling self-belief. And yet the simple pleasure which Ayrton Senna derived from winning, an unconfined joy which saw him, belts flung aside, almost bursting from the cockpit on his slowing-down lap, gave no hint of a ruthlessness which would give new meaning to winning at all costs.

To be sure, everyone was aware of his single-minded nature. Here was a Brazilian who had devoted all but the first four of his 25 years to becoming the best driver in the world. He had the natural speed to win championships in karts, Formula Ford, FF2000 and Formula 3. He was shrewd and totally determined, clever enough to realise that prodigious talent on its own was not sufficient; that it was necessary to ensure only the best equipment was available to him at all times. If sensibilities were hurt along the way, then so be it. He was a man with a mission and bruised feelings were not his problem.

That was fair enough in the mercenary world of Formula 1. Those who had banged wheels with Ayrton or tried unsuccessfully to tie him to a contract which was not to his liking were aware of his thinking. They may not have enjoyed the experience, but they understood it and, on quiet reflection, reluctantly admired it. All of that was known by the time he destroyed the opposition in Estoril.

This was his second season in Formula 1, the first having been spent with Toleman. Senna's three years with Lotus brought six wins, but not the championship he craved. Senna figured that McLaren could supply the necessary support in return for his links with Honda, the only obstacle being the presence of an equally shrewd and quick driver in the second car. Ayrton felt confident he could deal with Alain Prost.

They shared the winning in 1988, Senna scoring one victory more than the Frenchman and taking the title at the end of a year which had seen a reasonably harmonious relationship deteriorate. On a dry track, there was little to choose between the two – rain and qualifying laps being unquestionably in Senna's favour – but Ayrton met his match in Japan as they fought for the championship at the end of the following year.

Not prepared to be beaten under any circumstances, Senna lunged for a narrow gap which Prost, perhaps unwisely, had left open. The resulting collision between the two was to rip open the sometimes frightening side of Senna's nature. Sadly, it was to expose an unforgiving facet which would compromise an image of thrilling virtuosity as he raced into the Nineties.

Ayrton Senna's first Grand Prix win – a mesmerising
display of utter superiority in abominable conditions at
Estoril in 1985 – marked the start of a new era in
Formula 1.

The Eighties

AS the Eighties came to a close, Nigel Mansell had finally found the answer. After nine seasons of misery, misfortune, missed opportunities and moaning, the man with the Union Jack helmet was driving superbly. He had produced excellent performances in the past but, in 1989, he was happy. And it showed.

For a driver who not so much wears his heart on his sleeve as carries it around in a glass case for all to see, the effect of driving for Ferrari had a magical effect. Nigel was the undisputed *numero uno*, he had won his first race for the team and now he was lionised throughout Italy. He was a hero and, if the nation loved him, then so did everyone at Ferrari. And, the more they loved him, the better he drove. Nigel was relaxed, confident – and very quick.

It hadn't always been like that. Quick, yes. But relaxed and confident were words which did not spring easily to mind as you watched Mansell thrash around in a mire of persecution complexes and a desperate need to prove himself. Matters were not helped by the management at Lotus as they assumed control after Colin Chapman's death and inherited the legacy of what now seems the Lotus boss's foresight when it came to choosing a future British champion.

Chapman had the makings of a father-figure but the foster parents had neither the time nor the inclination to cope with the youngster's need for constant reassurance. When Frank Williams signed Mansell for 1985, it seemed he had made a drastic error of judgement but careful handling by team manager Peter Collins brought the best out in Mansell.

At the end of the season, Nigel won two Grands Prix on the trot. It may have taken 71 attempts to get that far, but now he was up and running. And quickly. As the world now knows, but for a punctured tyre in the final race of the following season, Nigel Mansell would have won the championship. It was a spectacular, dramatic and heart-rending finale. But, somehow, it was entirely appropriate, as was his exit on a stretcher from the penultimate round of the 1987 season as his title fight with team-mate Nelson Piquet came to a premature end.

The 1988 season was spent in limbo after Williams had lost the advantage of Honda power but Mansell was already on his way to Italy and the start of a relationship which would finally extract the very best from a thrilling if sometimes contorted talent. Then Ferrari signed Alain Prost for 1990 and Nigel's great dream was about to come to a temporary halt once more . . .

Mansell leads Alain Prost in the 1986 Australian
Grand Prix in Adelaide. The World Championship was
within the Williams driver's grasp when a puncture
snatched it from him.

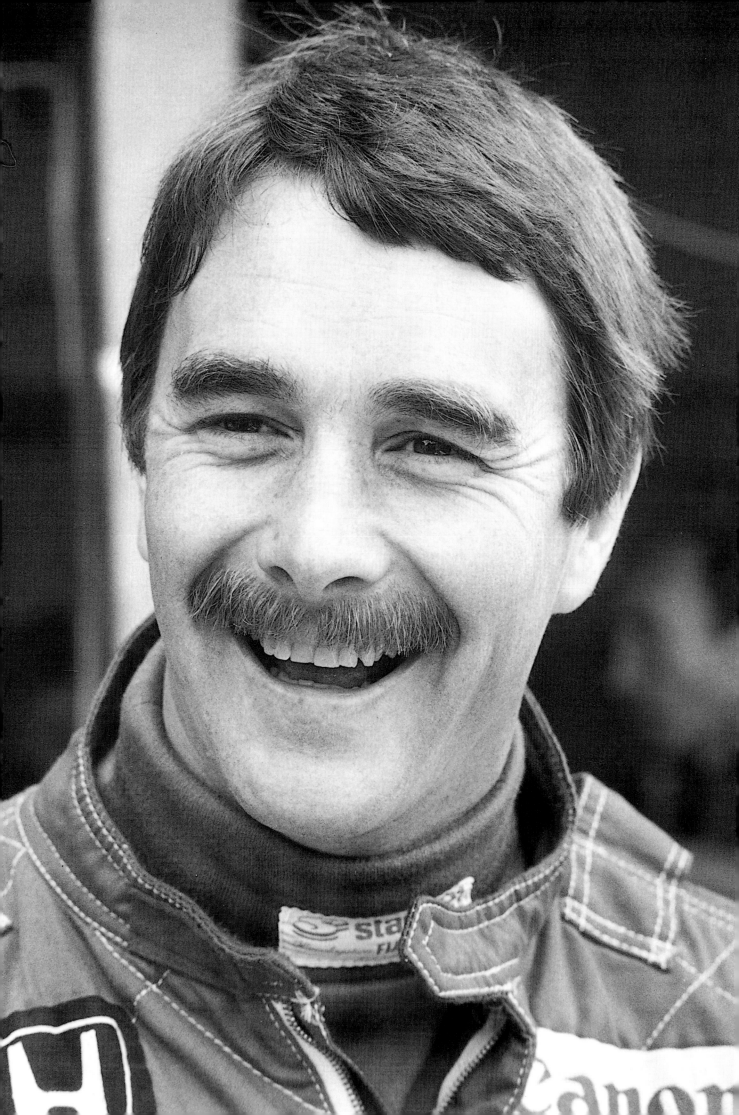

The Eighties

GERHARD Berger breezed into F1 during 1984 and drove the way he played. Not even a road accident at the end of the season would dent his infectious enthusiasm; indeed, it probably made him even more determined to enjoy life since he survived injuries – two broken vertebrae in his neck – which supposedly offered little chance of recovery. Having raced for the small ATS team, Gerhard was keen to drive for Arrows-BMW. He made it to the first race and did enough to persuade Benetton-BMW to sign him for 1986. On Pirelli tyres – when they were good, they were very good, which was not that often – Berger won his first Grand Prix in Mexico by keeping his head and running non-stop. It was an impressive and timely milestone since Gerhard had recently signed for Ferrari. Worries over his suitability for such a political hot-bed were unfounded and he wrapped up his first season with two victories. In 1988, he won at Monza – but not even that would change him. He continued to have fun but took his racing seriously enough to believe he was ready to run with Ayrton Senna at McLaren in 1990. For once, the ready smile would not be so evident . . .

HOW was it possible to come from Milan, drive for Ferrari, win Grands Prix – and be as equable and placid as Michele Alboreto? More to the point, how could you lose for Ferrari and yet keep your head while those around you in the national press appeared to be losing theirs?

Michele Alboreto understands his fellow Italians better than they understand themselves. His empathy converted into a mechanical sympathy while in the car. Mechanics marvelled at the state of his gearbox at the end of a hard race. You could hear the smooth gearchanges for yourself, see the flowing lines through the corners, witness a graceful fluency which was hammered into competitive shape by Ken Tyrrell.

Michele won races for Ken in Las Vegas and Detroit, and the Tyrrell mechanics still speak fondly of the shy, mop-topped young man who took the trouble to visit the team's headquarters and present each member of the workforce with a parting gift at the end of 1983. Alboreto returned to Tyrrell after his era with Ferrari was over – but it was the beginning of a sad end to a dignified career.

A delightful character, free from pretension and fond of espresso coffee and a quick cigarette, Alessandro Nannini graduated to Grand Prix racing in 1986 with Minardi, the low-key Italian team he had raced for in Formula 2 for three years. Success was never on the cards but Nannini's flair was obvious enough to attract the attention of Benetton, a logical connection in more ways than one given Benetton's Italian origins. Number two to Boutsen in 1988, Nannini nevertheless made the rostrum on two occasions. When the Belgian left to join Williams, Sandro became the mainstay of the team as number two drivers came and went. He rose to the task, finding the maturity and consistency which had been lacking, and was handily poised to accept his first win in Japan when Alain Prost and the race stewards combined to have Ayrton Senna removed from first place. Good fortune aside, Alessandro Nannini was widely tipped for long-term success as the Nineties beckoned. Tragically, his progress was halted with brutal suddenness when he lost his right arm in a helicopter crash towards the end of the following season. Surgeons succeeded in reattaching the severed limb and he was able to return to the circuits in touring car racing, but his F1 ambitions were at an end.

THIERRY Boutsen was proof that looks can be deceptive. Tall and lanky, the Belgian's gentle demeanour hid a steely determination on the track – but only when he had every confidence in the equipment. Quick and stylish, Boutsen was not given to throwing the car around unnecessarily but when the going was good he was unstoppable. He made his F1 debut with Arrows in 1983 and remained with the British team for three more years – perhaps a season too long since the results would never be forthcoming given the mediocre equipment put at his disposal – but a move to Benetton in 1987 did not provide all it promised even though Boutsen was the most consistent runner-up to the McLaren domination of 1988.

It was not until he switched to Williams the following year that Boutsen scored his first two wins with a pair of cool and precise drives in the rain in Canada and in Australia. Somehow, though, he was not developing into the consistent winner his earlier form had suggested. There was another victory in Hungary in 1990 but at the end of the year he was dropped from the team to accommodate the return of Nigel Mansell. Two frustrating seasons with Ligier eroded Thierry's reputation and a disheartening spell at Jordan brought down the curtain on his F1 career.

TEO FABI:
Only looked the part when he put on his crash helmet –
and even then he could be disappointing for no obvious
reason.

BRUNO GIACOMELLI:
Italian comedian who never quite got to grips with
Formula 1.

DEREK WARWICK:
Street-wise and a hard racer – but joining Renault was
the wrong move, even though it seemed right at the time.

STEFAN BELLOF:
A huge talent lost before it could be fully appreciated.

MARC SURER:
An excellent number two and a nice guy.

STEFAN JOHANSSON:
Bubbling personality who got the breaks but failed to make it.

EDDIE CHEEVER:
Been there and nearly done it – all at high speed.

PHILIPPE ALLIOT:
Cheerful French midfielder whose enthusiasm sometimes got the better of him.

SATORU NAKAJIMA:
Honda appointee who proved a worthy ambassador for
the company without posing a threat to his more highly
regarded team-mates.

ANDREA DE CESARIS:
Never won a race despite driving for almost every team in
the paddock.

IVAN CAPELLI:
Lots of good work in the Eighties, undone in the Nineties
by a nightmarish year at Ferrari.

MAURICIO GUGELMIN:
Swapping Formula 1 mediocrity
for Indy Car stardom?

THE NINETIES

By Steve Small

Ayrton Senna and Nigel Mansell continued their battles
into the Nineties. The iron-willed Brazilian resists
intense pressure from the Williams driver in the early
stages of the 1991 Belgian Grand Prix.

The Nineties

ONE distinguished motor racing journalist remarked to me that Senna had 'an elephant's memory', and if you incurred his displeasure in some way, by dint of word or pen, it was mentally filed away until some point in the future, when the Brazilian would make his feelings known. Certainly the personal hurt and injustice that Senna felt following his disqualification from the Japanese Grand Prix in 1989, and subsequent loss of the World Championship, was allowed to fester during the winter months and he entered the new decade in typically defiant mood. After much brinkmanship on all sides, a fudged 'apology' was accepted by FISA and the racing could begin. Ayrton's honour was still not satisfied, however, and retribution would be visited on Alain Prost later . . .

Certainly Senna's driving in 1990, when his McLaren-Honda was not as dominant as in the previous two seasons, showed him to be indisputably the greatest talent of the day. But still his intimidatory track manners sometimes went beyond the 'Marquess of Queensberry Rules' – as Sandro Nannini was to find in Hungary and Prost at Suzuka – as a second successive championship was decided in the most unsatisfactory, unsporting and potentially lethal manner.

It ill became a driver of such greatness to be involved in such tawdry practices and thankfully they were not to be seen in 1991 when his third championship was secured in the face of a stern challenge from Nigel Mansell and Williams-Renault. Making the most of an early-season points advantage gained by four straight wins, Ayrton, with but a couple of exceptions, wrung the absolute maximum from his McLaren-Honda V12 thereafter, and it could truly be said that the title was won more by the driver's extraordinary talents than the advantages inherent in the car.

Like Fangio before him, Senna knew that the best equipment would be needed if further titles were to be won, and his displeasure at McLaren's inability to supply it steadily grew. Outmanoeuvred by Prost, who secured the plum Williams ride for 1993, Senna was left to compete throughout the year in a car which was palpably inferior. But it gave the world the chance to savour some of the greatest driving seen in the modern era. Indeed his first-lap performance in the wet at Donington Park – when he swept past the four cars in front of him to take the lead – left the viewer literally agog. His end-of-year wins at Suzuka and Adelaide were no less dominant, leaving his competitors contemplating the awesome task that faced them with the Brazilian about to take up residence at Williams.

Imola–Senna. The two words are now inextricably linked. On 1 May 1994 Grand Prix racing lost one of its greatest figures, and a flawed genius joined the ranks of the immortals. Shocked and disbelieving, the world mourned, and a nation wept openly for one of its favourite sons.

Ayrton Senna's totally committed style made him almost
unbeatable on street circuits. He opened the 1991 season
with a dominant victory in the United States Grand Prix
at Phoenix.

The Nineties

A three-year contract with McLaren gave Berger the opportunity to confirm his status as a true championship contender hitherto denied him at Ferrari. Initially the lanky Austrian had to be shoehorned into a cockpit way too small, and the sheer pace of team-mate Ayrton Senna ultimately had a demoralising effect on the normally light-hearted Gerhard's performances. True, there were some fine drives – including three wins. But the way the first of these was handed to him by his team-mate like a favourite pet being tossed an unwanted morsel of food would have done little for any driver's self-esteem.

It was no surprise when, with a reportedly massive retainer dangled temptingly in front of him, Berger decided to return to the Scuderia and help in the massive task of rebuilding a team still striving to recapture former glories. It was to be a nightmarish first season, during which serious question marks were raised as to whether his best days were behind him. Happily his true stature was restored in 1994, which not only saw him overcome huge personal grief at the loss of both Senna and Ratzenberger at Imola, but show great maturity off the track as the sport's senior driver. His win at Hockenheim was undoubtedly the most popular of the year, reflecting the affection in which he has long been held.

NOT many Grand Prix drivers get to enjoy an Indian Summer. Once on the way down it's usually free-fall through to the back of the grid and – if they're lucky – employment in a less pressured and glamorous form of the sport. But Patrese thoroughly deserved to bask in the achievements of his 1991 season when he was often as competitive as team-mate Mansell. Wins in Mexico and Portugal were fitting reward for his hard work during the previous two years developing the Williams-Renault package to its championship-chasing pitch. So highly was Riccardo thought of by all at Didcot that it was a bemused Boutsen who was shown the door when Mansell's return was imminent. The decision was richly repaid by the loyal and unstinting service Patrese continued to give, even if somewhat less effectively in his final year when the FW14B seemed less to his liking.

Nevertheless there was one final victory in Japan for the Italian to savour, and second place in the World Championship underlined his admirable consistency. It would have been a good place to draw a line under a phenomenally long F1 career, for his final season at Benetton was a disappointing one. After more than 250 Grands Prix, it was time for Riccardo to leave the circuits to the younger lions, still hungry for success.

The Nineties

MANSELL'S love affair with Ferrari and all things Italian was indeed to turn sour with the arrival of Alain Prost at the beginning of 1990. Gushing bonhomie was soon replaced by mid-season disaffection, and the shock announcement of *Il Leone*'s threat to take end-of-season retirement.

Salvation was at hand in the unlikely shape of a return to Didcot, where the parting of the ways had hardly been amicable and many of the team's personnel were less than thrilled at the thought of Nigel's return. Nevertheless, having developed the car and engine to a point where they could match the McLaren-Honda, Williams-Renault sorely needed his talents to actually secure the championship.

That it did not happen in 1991 was due in part to a blighted early-season run of races where technical problems robbed Mansell of much-needed points. Nigel for his part drove superbly, often all but matching the brilliance of Senna, and he certainly carried the fight to the Brazilian in a typically no-holds-barred manner which, on occasions, brought back memories of their mid-Eighties clashes. The following season indisputably belonged to Nigel as he soundly thrashed the opposition in a car which had no peer but, crucially, did it with all the style and commitment that had long since become his trademark. Forget the over-exuberant partisanship of a minority of idiotic fans who invaded the Silverstone circuit, for Nigel's cult following had become truly global, his legion of worshippers relishing the 'British Bulldog' style and his thrilling performances.

Much to their disappointment, they were denied the chance to savour the prospect of a second successive championship triumph. Mid-season contract wranglings dragged on to the point where Nigel, unwilling to accept the arrival of Alain Prost for 1993, was eventually left with no viable alternative but to defect to Indy Car racing. Not a little hurt at his treatment, Mansell headed across the Atlantic with embittered parting shots at the form of the sport which had brought him so much. Certainly Formula 1 was the loser, while the credibility of Indy Car racing gained an immense boost with the participation of the reigning World Champion, who brought with him a whole new audience for the North American series.

Typically, Mansell defied the critics who warned of impending disaster on the ovals, forcing them to eat their words. He not only won the PPG Indy Car World Series for Newman-Haas but also dented the standing of many a hitherto vaunted competitor in this sphere of racing. The Stateside honeymoon was to be brief, however. A disastrous second year, totally dominated by Penske, yielded not a single win and Nigel quickly lost interest, especially when, in the wake of Ayrton Senna's death, Bernie Ecclestone engineered his part-time return to the Grand Prix ranks with Williams. Four highly priced, but inconclusive, appearances yielded an end-of-season win in Adelaide.

It was not enough to gain him the drive for 1995 but, ever confident of his worth, Mansell negotiated himself yet another lucrative contract, this time with a McLaren team desperate for success. But with his new car proving less competitive than he expected, his motivation, for so long a key factor in his achievements, rapidly evaporated and his illustrious career now seems to be at an end.

Mansell's Magic! The rapturous devotion of the
Silverstone crowd is summed up by a trackside banner as
their homespun hero sweeps to victory in the 1991 British
Grand Prix.

The Nineties

AS the Nineties began, Alain Prost had regained his crown but – crucially – lost his kingdom. Driven from his beloved McLaren by Ayrton Senna, he took his number one to Ferrari in the hope that a new alliance could be forged on foreign soil which would overcome his former allies. Initially the partnership went well. Prost's fabled testing ability and huge technical knowledge proved an immense asset, while his super-smooth driving technique remained formidably effective. In 'The Professor' Ferrari had hired a man with an analytical brain as well as one of the world's greatest drivers, but he was also a seasoned campaigner who had acquired a great deal of political savvy. This soon enabled him to become the fulcrum of the team since, for all Mansell's good work in 1989, his thrilling if rather bludgeoning approach paid off only intermittently. It very nearly worked out for Prost, whose chances of a fourth title disappeared when he found himself deposited in the Suzuka gravel trap courtesy of Ayrton Senna.

It had been a season of much achievement but, typically perhaps, Ferrari rested on their laurels over the winter months. Prost was emphatically not guilty of such complacency and campaigned vehemently for a new chassis and various other changes behind the scenes. The political intrigue took its toll as the season wore on and, despite some excellent performances when the car allowed, Alain's criticism of the team grew ever louder. He paid the price for his frankness with one race remaining, leaving him without a competitive drive for 1992.

Prost opted to take a sabbatical and it proved to be a wise choice, for he sowed the seeds early for his inclusion in the Williams-Renault line-up the following year, thus frustrating the ambitions of his deadly rival Senna, who was now casting covetous eyes in that direction. Not only was Senna blocked out, but Nigel Mansell, the incumbent and World Champion-elect no less, also contrived to parley his way out of the team, such were his forebodings at the prospect of the Frenchman's arrival. Thus the field was left clear for Alain as he brought his still wonderful driving talents back to the circuits for one final and triumphant season.

Many see 1993 as a rather dull year with Prost winning seven races in characteristically unobtrusive manner, largely by virtue of having the best car by some margin. However, in any walk of life everyone has their own way of doing things, and Alain Prost's brand of subtlety and racecraft appealed to the connoisseurs of the sport who rejoiced to see precision, style, economy and mechanical empathy reap their just rewards. In a career that spanned 199 actual race starts with 51 wins (a success ratio of more than one in four) he amassed a staggering 798.5 points (equivalent to third place in every race). Yes, Prost is truly one of 'The Greats'.

Alain Prost's second season at Ferrari saw him fail to win
a race for the first time in a decade. The Frenchman's
frustration at the team's lack of competitiveness made a
split almost inevitable.

L EAF through the pages of this book and look at some of the greats of the early years: Gonzalez, Ascari and Fangio. Their physiques could be described as stocky, if not portly, and certainly they were beefy men endowed with the strength needed to handle the unsophisticated but powerful front-engined machines of the day. The current World Champion, Michael Schumacher, quite apart from his immense natural skills, is also widely regarded as the fittest physical specimen on the Grand Prix scene today, his body as finely honed as the svelte Benetton he drives with such brilliance on the track. This point is made to show just how far Grand Prix racing has progressed during the past five decades: drivers are now athletes in the true sense of the word.

Schumacher's raw talent, once spotted, has been systematically groomed for success in a way that, say, even Senna's was not, only a decade or so earlier. This may in some way explain why the polite but slightly formal – and some contend occasionally arrogant – German has not found his way into the heart of every fan, for all his refreshing enthusiasm.

Michael's eye-catching Grand Prix debut for Jordan at Spa in 1991 saw him swiftly signed up and whisked off to Benetton, where he has become the key figure in the team's rise to the pinnacle of the Grand Prix world. As a driver it soon became apparent that here was a special talent, making occasional mistakes but rarely repeating them. Equally at home on any type of circuit in any conditions, wet or dry, and displaying a Senna-like ruthlessness on the track when dealing with back-markers, Schumacher rapidly progressed during his first two seasons to the position of pretender to the Brazilian's throne. Sadly the black weekend at Imola in 1994 saw the crown pass to him in the worst way possible; in the previous two races it had been clear that Michael had the car and the confidence in his own abilities to stretch even Ayrton's talents to the full.

The championship, though inevitably devalued, still had to be won and, with a mixture of brilliance and a good measure of controversy, it was. Despite disqualifications in Britain and Belgium, which meant the removal of 16 points, and a two-race ban, the 25-year-old was clearly the man to beat, even if suspicions lurked as to the legality of his car. The final showdown in Australia, when he collided with Damon Hill and thus confirmed his crown, was an unsatisfactory, if somehow perversely fitting, way to end a season of disarray for Formula 1. The pressures on the German will inevitably grow, but the opportunity now lies ahead for him to confirm his position as the world's best driver and make an even greater mark as Grand Prix racing enters a new era.

The stylish assurance with which Michael Schumacher
outpaced the McLarens of Ayrton Senna and Gerhard
Berger in the 1992 Spanish Grand Prix confirmed his rich
potential.

THE World Championship crown has generally been the domain of the absolute greats, from Fangio through to Senna. But there were also years when it went to less vaunted, though still *very* talented, drivers such as Phil Hill, Denny Hulme and – yes – Graham Hill. So for Damon to follow in his father's footsteps and claim the sport's ultimate accolade *is* a realistic proposition, especially if he continues to display the scintillating form he showed in the last half of the 1994 season, when he all but overtook Schumacher's points total, and the early part of 1995, when the latest Williams-Renault looked the car to beat.

The sheer good sense and immense determination shown by Hill since his elevation from his role as a largely unregarded test driver to the Williams race team have brought rewards aplenty. In 35 starts to date for the Didcot outfit, Damon has scored 11 wins and amassed 180 points.

Off-track, his down-to-earth attitude and dignified handling of the huge disappointment of losing the chance of the 1994 title in Adelaide won him many admirers. Behind the wheel, Damon has proved he can do the job, cut it with the best and beat them. With the little bit of luck every driver needs, a thoroughly well-deserved World Championship could be his . . .

MARTIN BRUNDLE:
Still an asset to any team – and a career
deserving of a win.

JEAN ALESI:
Alesi expects, and Ferrari must surely deliver.

MIKA HÄKKINEN:
Now showing guile to go with his undoubted speed.

DAVID COULTHARD:
Utterly confident of his own abilities.

MARK BLUNDELL:
Doesn't mess about – deserves a place on the grid.

PIERLUIGI MARTINI:
Been around for ages – now past his sell-by date.

ROBERTO MORENO:
One big chance, otherwise consigned to the underclass.

STEFANO MODENA:
Natural talent unhappy in the Grand Prix firmament.

ERIC BERNARD:
Despite recent comeback, a broken leg in 1991
torpedoed his chances.

J.J. LEHTO:
Broken resistance, and broken dreams.

NICOLA LARINI:
Little chance to show his considerable ability.

JOHNNY HERBERT:
Highly rated for so long, but must now perform.

HEINZ-HARALD FRENTZEN:
Talent now blossoming after chequered apprenticeship
in lower formulae.

EDDIE IRVINE:
Refreshing non-conformist attitude,
both on and off the track. But for how long?

RUBENS BARRICHELLO:
Bright, light-hearted Brazilian now more serious after
tasting the downside of Formula 1.

KARL WENDLINGER:
Impressive progress until serious injury. Now facing an
uphill task to regain his previous form.

MICHAEL ANDRETTI:
Formula 1 now just a bad dream.

JOS VERSTAPPEN:
Impressive achievements despite very limited
racing history.

OLIVIER PANIS:
Hoping to succeed where so many of his
compatriots have failed.

MIKA SALO:
Latest hot-shot – will need a cool head.

1950 *Champion: Giuseppe Farina*

Race	Circuit	Driver	Car
British GP	Silverstone	Giuseppe Farina	Alfa Romeo 158
Monaco GP	Monte Carlo	Juan Manuel Fangio	Alfa Romeo 158
Swiss GP	Bremgarten	Giuseppe Farina	Alfa Romeo 158
Belgian GP	Spa-Francorchamps	Juan Manuel Fangio	Alfa Romeo 158
French GP	Reims	Juan Manuel Fangio	Alfa Romeo 158
Italian GP	Monza	Giuseppe Farina	Alfa Romeo 158

1951 *Champion: Juan Manuel Fangio*

Swiss GP	Bremgarten	Juan Manuel Fangio	Alfa Romeo 158
Belgian GP	Spa-Francorchamps	Giuseppe Farina	Alfa Romeo 158
French GP	Reims	Juan Manuel Fangio/ Luigi Fagioli	Alfa Romeo 158
British GP	Silverstone	Froilan Gonzalez	Ferrari 375
German GP	Nürburgring	Alberto Ascari	Ferrari 375
Italian GP	Monza	Alberto Ascari	Ferrari 375
Spanish GP	Pedralbes	Juan Manuel Fangio	Alfa Romeo 159

1952 *Champion: Alberto Ascari*

Swiss GP	Bremgarten	Piero Taruffi	Ferrari 500
Belgian GP	Spa-Francorchamps	Alberto Ascari	Ferrari 500
French GP	Rouen	Alberto Ascari	Ferrari 500
British GP	Silverstone	Alberto Ascari	Ferrari 500
German GP	Nürburgring	Alberto Ascari	Ferrari 500
Dutch GP	Zandvoort	Alberto Ascari	Ferrari 500
Italian GP	Monza	Alberto Ascari	Ferrari 500

1953 *Champion: Alberto Ascari*

Argentinian GP	Buenos Aires	Alberto Ascari	Ferrari 500
Dutch GP	Zandvoort	Alberto Ascari	Ferrari 500
Belgian GP	Spa-Francorchamps	Alberto Ascari	Ferrari 500
French GP	Reims	Mike Hawthorn	Ferrari 500
British GP	Silverstone	Alberto Ascari	Ferrari 500
German GP	Nürburgring	Giuseppe Farina	Ferrari 500
Swiss GP	Bremgarten	Alberto Ascari	Ferrari 500
Italian GP	Monza	Juan Manuel Fangio	Maserati A6GCM/53

1954 *Champion: Juan Manuel Fangio*

Argentinian GP	Buenos Aires	Juan Manuel Fangio	Maserati 250F
Belgian GP	Spa-Francorchamps	Juan Manuel Fangio	Maserati 250F
French GP	Reims	Juan Manuel Fangio	Mercedes-Benz W196
British GP	Silverstone	Froilan Gonzalez	Ferrari 625
German GP	Nürburgring	Juan Manuel Fangio	Mercedes-Benz W196
Swiss GP	Bremgarten	Juan Manuel Fangio	Mercedes-Benz W196
Italian GP	Monza	Juan Manuel Fangio	Mercedes-Benz W196
Spanish GP	Pedralbes	Mike Hawthorn	Ferrari 553/555

1955 *Champion: Juan Manuel Fangio*

Argentinian GP	Buenos Aires	Juan Manuel Fangio	Mercedes-Benz W196
Monaco GP	Monte Carlo	Maurice Trintignant	Ferrari 625
Belgian GP	Spa-Francorchamps	Juan Manuel Fangio	Mercedes-Benz W196
Dutch GP	Zandvoort	Juan Manuel Fangio	Mercedes-Benz W196
British GP	Aintree	Stirling Moss	Mercedes-Benz W196
Italian GP	Monza	Juan Manuel Fangio	Mercedes-Benz W196

1956 *Champion: Juan Manuel Fangio*

Argentinian GP	Buenos Aires	Juan Manuel Fangio/ Luigi Musso	Lancia-Ferrari D50
Monaco GP	Monte Carlo	Stirling Moss	Maserati 250F
Belgian GP	Spa-Francorchamps	Peter Collins	Lancia-Ferrari D50A
French GP	Reims	Peter Collins	Lancia-Ferrari D50A
British GP	Silverstone	Juan Manuel Fangio	Lancia-Ferrari D50A
German GP	Nürburgring	Juan Manuel Fangio	Lancia-Ferrari D50A
Italian GP	Monza	Stirling Moss	Maserati 250F

1957 *Champion: Juan Manuel Fangio*

Argentinian GP	Buenos Aires	Juan Manuel Fangio	Maserati 250F
Monaco GP	Monte Carlo	Juan Manuel Fangio	Maserati 250F
French GP	Rouen	Juan Manuel Fangio	Maserati 250F
British GP	Aintree	Stirling Moss/ Tony Brooks	Vanwall
German GP	Nürburgring	Juan Manuel Fangio	Maserati 250F
Pescara GP	Pescara	Stirling Moss	Vanwall
Italian GP	Monza	Stirling Moss	Vanwall

1958 *Champion: Mike Hawthorn*

Argentinian GP	Buenos Aires	Stirling Moss	Cooper T43-Climax
Monaco GP	Monte Carlo	Maurice Trintignant	Cooper T45-Climax
Dutch GP	Zandvoort	Stirling Moss	Vanwall
Belgian GP	Spa-Francorchamps	Tony Brooks	Vanwall
French GP	Reims	Mike Hawthorn	Ferrari 246
British GP	Silverstone	Peter Collins	Ferrari 246
German GP	Nürburgring	Tony Brooks	Vanwall
Portuguese GP	Oporto	Stirling Moss	Vanwall
Italian GP	Monza	Tony Brooks	Vanwall
Moroccan GP	Casablanca	Stirling Moss	Vanwall

1959 *Champion: Jack Brabham*

Monaco GP	Monte Carlo	Jack Brabham	Cooper T51-Climax
Dutch GP	Zandvoort	Joakim Bonnier	BRM 25
French GP	Reims	Tony Brooks	Ferrari 246
British GP	Aintree	Jack Brabham	Cooper T51-Climax
German GP	AVUS	Tony Brooks	Ferrari 246
Portuguese GP	Monsanto	Stirling Moss	Cooper T51-Climax
Italian GP	Monza	Stirling Moss	Cooper T51-Climax
US GP	Sebring	Bruce McLaren	Cooper T51-Climax

1960 *Champion: Jack Brabham*

Argentinian GP	Buenos Aires	Bruce McLaren	Cooper T51-Climax
Monaco GP	Monte Carlo	Stirling Moss	Lotus 18-Climax
Dutch GP	Zandvoort	Jack Brabham	Cooper T53-Climax
Belgian GP	Spa-Francorchamps	Jack Brabham	Cooper T53-Climax
French GP	Reims	Jack Brabham	Cooper T53-Climax
British GP	Silverstone	Jack Brabham	Cooper T53-Climax
Portuguese GP	Oporto	Jack Brabham	Cooper T53-Climax
Italian GP	Monza	Phil Hill	Ferrari 246
US GP	Riverside	Stirling Moss	Lotus 18-Climax

1961 *Champion: Phil Hill*

Monaco GP	Monte Carlo	Stirling Moss	Lotus 18-Climax
Dutch GP	Zandvoort	Wolfgang von Trips	Ferrari 156
Belgian GP	Spa-Francorchamps	Phil Hill	Ferrari 156
French GP	Reims	Giancarlo Baghetti	Ferrari 156
British GP	Aintree	Wolfgang von Trips	Ferrari 156
German GP	Nürburgring	Stirling Moss	Lotus 18/21-Climax
Italian GP	Monza	Phil Hill	Ferrari 156
US GP	Watkins Glen	Innes Ireland	Lotus 21-Climax

1962 *Champion: Graham Hill*

Dutch GP	Zandvoort	Graham Hill	BRM P578
Monaco GP	Monte Carlo	Bruce McLaren	Cooper T60-Climax
Belgian GP	Spa-Francorchamps	Jim Clark	Lotus 25-Climax
French GP	Rouen	Dan Gurney	Porsche 804
British GP	Aintree	Jim Clark	Lotus 25-Climax
German GP	Nürburgring	Graham Hill	BRM P578
Italian GP	Monza	Graham Hill	BRM P578
US GP	Watkins Glen	Jim Clark	Lotus 25-Climax
South African GP	East London	Graham Hill	BRM P578

1963 *Champion: Jim Clark*

Monaco GP	Monte Carlo	Graham Hill	BRM P578
Belgian GP	Spa-Francorchamps	Jim Clark	Lotus 25-Climax
Dutch GP	Zandvoort	Jim Clark	Lotus 25-Climax
French GP	Reims	Jim Clark	Lotus 25-Climax
British GP	Silverstone	Jim Clark	Lotus 25-Climax
German GP	Nürburgring	John Surtees	Ferrari 156
Italian GP	Monza	Jim Clark	Lotus 25-Climax
US GP	Watkins Glen	Graham Hill	BRM P578
Mexican GP	Mexico City	Jim Clark	Lotus 25-Climax
South African GP	East London	Jim Clark	Lotus 25-Climax

1964 *Champion: John Surtees*

Monaco GP	Monte Carlo	Graham Hill	BRM P261
Dutch GP	Zandvoort	Jim Clark	Lotus 25-Climax
Belgian GP	Spa-Francorchamps	Jim Clark	Lotus 25-Climax
French GP	Rouen	Dan Gurney	Brabham BT7-Climax
British GP	Brands Hatch	Jim Clark	Lotus 25-Climax
German GP	Nürburgring	John Surtees	Ferrari 158
Austrian GP	Zeltweg	Lorenzo Bandini	Ferrari 156
Italian GP	Monza	John Surtees	Ferrari 158
US GP	Watkins Glen	Graham Hill	BRM P261
Mexican GP	Mexico City	Dan Gurney	Brabham BT7-Climax

1965 *Champion: Jim Clark*

South African GP	East London	Jim Clark	Lotus 33-Climax
Monaco GP	Monte Carlo	Graham Hill	BRM P261
Belgian GP	Spa-Francorchamps	Jim Clark	Lotus 33-Climax
French GP	Clermont Ferrand	Jim Clark	Lotus 33-Climax
British GP	Silverstone	Jim Clark	Lotus 33-Climax
Dutch GP	Zandvoort	Jim Clark	Lotus 33-Climax
German GP	Nürburgring	Jim Clark	Lotus 33-Climax
Italian GP	Monza	Jackie Stewart	BRM P261
US GP	Watkins Glen	Graham Hill	BRM P261
Mexican GP	Mexico City	Richie Ginther	Honda RA272

1966 *Champion: Jack Brabham*

Monaco GP	Monte Carlo	**Jackie Stewart**	BRM P261
Belgian GP	Spa-Francorchamps	**John Surtees**	Ferrari 312
French GP	Reims	**Jack Brabham**	Brabham BT19-Repco
British GP	Brands Hatch	**Jack Brabham**	Brabham BT19-Repco
Dutch GP	Zandvoort	**Jack Brabham**	Brabham BT19-Repco
German GP	Nürburgring	**Jack Brabham**	Brabham BT19-Repco
Italian GP	Monza	**Ludovico Scarfiotti**	Ferrari 312
US GP	Watkins Glen	**Jim Clark**	Lotus 43-BRM
Mexican GP	Mexico City	**John Surtees**	Cooper T81-Maserati

1967 *Champion: Denny Hulme*

South African GP	Kyalami	**Pedro Rodriguez**	Cooper T81-Maserati
Monaco GP	Monte Carlo	**Denny Hulme**	Brabham BT20-Repco
Dutch GP	Zandvoort	**Jim Clark**	Lotus 49-Cosworth
Belgian GP	Spa-Francorchamps	**Dan Gurney**	Eagle T1G-Weslake
French GP	Le Mans	**Jack Brabham**	Brabham BT24-Repco
British GP	Silverstone	**Jim Clark**	Lotus 49-Cosworth
German GP	Nürburgring	**Denny Hulme**	Brabham BT24-Repco
Canadian GP	Mosport	**Jack Brabham**	Brabham BT24-Repco
Italian GP	Monza	**John Surtees**	Honda RA300
US GP	Watkins Glen	**Jim Clark**	Lotus 49-Cosworth
Mexican GP	Mexico City	**Jim Clark**	Lotus 49-Cosworth

1968 *Champion: Graham Hill*

South African GP	Kyalami	**Jim Clark**	Lotus 49-Cosworth
Spanish GP	Jarama	**Graham Hill**	Lotus 49-Cosworth
Monaco GP	Monte Carlo	**Graham Hill**	Lotus 49B-Cosworth
Belgian GP	Spa-Francorchamps	**Bruce McLaren**	McLaren M7A-Cosworth
Dutch GP	Zandvoort	**Jackie Stewart**	Matra MS10-Cosworth
French GP	Rouen	**Jacky Ickx**	Ferrari 312
British GP	Brands Hatch	**Jo Siffert**	Lotus 49B-Cosworth
German GP	Nürburgring	**Jackie Stewart**	Matra MS10-Cosworth
Italian GP	Monza	**Denny Hulme**	McLaren M7A-Cosworth
Canadian GP	Mont-Tremblant	**Denny Hulme**	McLaren M7A-Cosworth
US GP	Watkins Glen	**Jackie Stewart**	Matra MS10-Cosworth
Mexican GP	Mexico City	**Graham Hill**	Lotus 49B-Cosworth

1969 *Champion: Jackie Stewart*

South African GP	Kyalami	**Jackie Stewart**	Matra MS10-Cosworth
Spanish GP	Montjuich	**Jackie Stewart**	Matra MS80-Cosworth
Monaco GP	Monte Carlo	**Graham Hill**	Lotus 49B-Cosworth
Dutch GP	Zandvoort	**Jackie Stewart**	Matra MS80-Cosworth
French GP	Clermont Ferrand	**Jackie Stewart**	Matra MS80-Cosworth
British GP	Silverstone	**Jackie Stewart**	Matra MS80-Cosworth
German GP	Nürburgring	**Jacky Ickx**	Brabham BT26A-Cosworth
Italian GP	Monza	**Jackie Stewart**	Matra MS80-Cosworth
Canadian GP	Mosport	**Jacky Ickx**	Brabham BT26A-Cosworth
US GP	Watkins Glen	**Jochen Rindt**	Lotus 49B-Cosworth
Mexican GP	Mexico City	**Denny Hulme**	McLaren M7A-Cosworth

1970 *Champion: Jochen Rindt*

South African GP	Kyalami	**Jack Brabham**	Brabham BT33-Cosworth
Spanish GP	Jarama	**Jackie Stewart**	March 701-Cosworth
Monaco GP	Monte Carlo	**Jochen Rindt**	Lotus 49C-Cosworth
Belgian GP	Spa-Francorchamps	**Pedro Rodriguez**	BRM P153
Dutch GP	Zandvoort	**Jochen Rindt**	Lotus 72-Cosworth
French GP	Clermont Ferrand	**Jochen Rindt**	Lotus 72-Cosworth
British GP	Brands Hatch	**Jochen Rindt**	Lotus 72-Cosworth
German GP	Hockenheim	**Jochen Rindt**	Lotus 72-Cosworth
Austrian GP	Österreichring	**Jacky Ickx**	Ferrari 312B
Italian GP	Monza	**Clay Regazzoni**	Ferrari 312B
Canadian GP	Mont-Tremblant	**Jacky Ickx**	Ferrari 312B
US GP	Watkins Glen	**Emerson Fittipaldi**	Lotus 72-Cosworth
Mexican GP	Mexico City	**Jacky Ickx**	Ferrari 312B

1971 *Champion: Jackie Stewart*

South African GP	Kyalami	**Mario Andretti**	Ferrari 312B
Spanish GP	Montjuich	**Jackie Stewart**	Tyrrell 003-Cosworth
Monaco GP	Monte Carlo	**Jackie Stewart**	Tyrrell 003-Cosworth
Dutch GP	Zandvoort	**Jacky Ickx**	Ferrari 312B
French GP	Paul Ricard	**Jackie Stewart**	Tyrrell 003-Cosworth
British GP	Silverstone	**Jackie Stewart**	Tyrrell 003-Cosworth
German GP	Nürburgring	**Jackie Stewart**	Tyrrell 003-Cosworth
Austrian GP	Österreichring	**Jo Siffert**	BRM P160
Italian GP	Monza	**Peter Gethin**	BRM P160
Canadian GP	Mosport	**Jackie Stewart**	Tyrrell 003-Cosworth
US GP	Watkins Glen	**François Cevert**	Tyrrell 002-Cosworth

1972 *Champion: Emerson Fittipaldi*

Argentinian GP	Buenos Aires	**Jackie Stewart**	Tyrrell 003-Cosworth
South African GP	Kyalami	**Denny Hulme**	McLaren M19A-Cosworth
Spanish GP	Jarama	**Emerson Fittipaldi**	Lotus 72-Cosworth
Monaco GP	Monte Carlo	**Jean-Pierre Beltoise**	BRM P160
Belgian GP	Nivelles	**Emerson Fittipaldi**	Lotus 72-Cosworth
French GP	Clermont Ferrand	**Jackie Stewart**	Tyrrell 003-Cosworth
British GP	Brands Hatch	**Emerson Fittipaldi**	Lotus 72-Cosworth
German GP	Nürburgring	**Jacky Ickx**	Ferrari 312B
Austrian GP	Österreichring	**Emerson Fittipaldi**	Lotus 72-Cosworth
Italian GP	Monza	**Emerson Fittipaldi**	Lotus 72-Cosworth
Canadian GP	Mosport	**Jackie Stewart**	Tyrrell 005-Cosworth
US GP	Watkins Glen	**Jackie Stewart**	Tyrrell 005-Cosworth

1973 *Champion: Jackie Stewart*

Argentinian GP	Buenos Aires	**Emerson Fittipaldi**	Lotus 72-Cosworth
Brazilian GP	Interlagos	**Emerson Fittipaldi**	Lotus 72-Cosworth
South African GP	Kyalami	**Jackie Stewart**	Tyrrell 006-Cosworth
Spanish GP	Montjuich	**Emerson Fittipaldi**	Lotus 72-Cosworth
Belgian GP	Zolder	**Jackie Stewart**	Tyrrell 006-Cosworth
Monaco GP	Monte Carlo	**Jackie Stewart**	Tyrrell 006-Cosworth
Swedish GP	Anderstorp	**Denny Hulme**	McLaren M23-Cosworth
French GP	Paul Ricard	**Ronnie Peterson**	Lotus 72-Cosworth
British GP	Silverstone	**Peter Revson**	McLaren M23-Cosworth
Dutch GP	Zandvoort	**Jackie Stewart**	Tyrrell 006-Cosworth
German GP	Nürburgring	**Jackie Stewart**	Tyrrell 006-Cosworth
Austrian GP	Österreichring	**Ronnie Peterson**	Lotus 72-Cosworth
Italian GP	Monza	**Ronnie Peterson**	Lotus 72-Cosworth
Canadian GP	Mosport	**Peter Revson**	McLaren M23-Cosworth
US GP	Watkins Glen	**Ronnie Peterson**	Lotus 72-Cosworth

1974 *Champion: Emerson Fittipaldi*

Argentinian GP	Buenos Aires	**Denny Hulme**	McLaren M23-Cosworth
Brazilian GP	Interlagos	**Emerson Fittipaldi**	McLaren M23-Cosworth
South African GP	Kyalami	**Carlos Reutemann**	Brabham BT44-Cosworth
Spanish GP	Jarama	**Niki Lauda**	Ferrari 312B3
Belgian GP	Nivelles	**Emerson Fittipaldi**	McLaren M23-Cosworth
Monaco GP	Monte Carlo	**Ronnie Peterson**	Lotus 72-Cosworth
Swedish GP	Anderstorp	**Jody Scheckter**	Tyrrell 007-Cosworth
Dutch GP	Zandvoort	**Niki Lauda**	Ferrari 312B3
French GP	Dijon-Prenois	**Ronnie Peterson**	Lotus 72-Cosworth
British GP	Brands Hatch	**Jody Scheckter**	Tyrrell 007-Cosworth
German GP	Nürburgring	**Clay Regazzoni**	Ferrari 312B3
Austrian GP	Österreichring	**Carlos Reutemann**	Brabham BT44-Cosworth
Italian GP	Monza	**Ronnie Peterson**	Lotus 72-Cosworth
Canadian GP	Mosport	**Emerson Fittipaldi**	McLaren M23-Cosworth
US GP	Watkins Glen	**Carlos Reutemann**	Brabham BT44-Cosworth

1975 *Champion: Niki Lauda*

Argentinian GP	Buenos Aires	**Emerson Fittipaldi**	McLaren M23-Cosworth
Brazilian GP	Interlagos	**Carlos Pace**	Brabham BT44B-Cosworth
South African GP	Kyalami	**Jody Scheckter**	Tyrrell 007-Cosworth
Spanish GP	Montjuich	**Jochen Mass**	McLaren M23-Cosworth
Monaco GP	Monte Carlo	**Niki Lauda**	Ferrari 312T
Belgian GP	Zolder	**Niki Lauda**	Ferrari 312T
Swedish GP	Anderstorp	**Niki Lauda**	Ferrari 312T
Dutch GP	Zandvoort	**James Hunt**	Hesketh 308-Cosworth
French GP	Paul Ricard	**Niki Lauda**	Ferrari 312T
British GP	Silverstone	**Emerson Fittipaldi**	McLaren M23-Cosworth
German GP	Nürburgring	**Carlos Reutemann**	Brabham BT44B-Cosworth
Austrian GP	Österreichring	**Vittorio Brambilla**	March 751-Cosworth
Italian GP	Monza	**Clay Regazzoni**	Ferrari 312T
US GP	Watkins Glen	**Niki Lauda**	Ferrari 312T

1976 *Champion: James Hunt*

Brazilian GP	Interlagos	**Niki Lauda**	Ferrari 312T
South African GP	Kyalami	**Niki Lauda**	Ferrari 312T
US (West) GP	Long Beach	**Clay Regazzoni**	Ferrari 312T
Spanish GP	Jarama	**James Hunt**	McLaren M23-Cosworth
Belgian GP	Zolder	**Niki Lauda**	Ferrari 312T2
Monaco GP	Monte Carlo	**Niki Lauda**	Ferrari 312T2
Swedish GP	Anderstorp	**Jody Scheckter**	Tyrrell P34-Cosworth
French GP	Paul Ricard	**James Hunt**	McLaren M23-Cosworth
British GP	Brands Hatch	**Niki Lauda**	Ferrari 312T2
German GP	Nürburgring	**James Hunt**	McLaren M23-Cosworth
Austrian GP	Österreichring	**John Watson**	Penske PC4-Cosworth
Dutch GP	Zandvoort	**James Hunt**	McLaren M23-Cosworth
Italian GP	Monza	**Ronnie Peterson**	March 761-Cosworth
Canadian GP	Mosport	**James Hunt**	McLaren M23-Cosworth
US (East) GP	Watkins Glen	**James Hunt**	McLaren M23-Cosworth
Japanese GP	Mount Fuji	**Mario Andretti**	Lotus 77-Cosworth

1977 *Champion: Niki Lauda*

Argentinian GP	Buenos Aires	**Jody Scheckter**	Wolf WR1-Cosworth
Brazilian GP	Interlagos	**Carlos Reutemann**	Ferrari 312T2
South African GP	Kyalami	**Niki Lauda**	Ferrari 312T2
US (West) GP	Long Beach	**Mario Andretti**	Lotus 78-Cosworth

1977 (continued)

Race	Circuit	Driver	Car
Spanish GP	Jarama	Mario Andretti	Lotus 78-Cosworth
Monaco GP	Monte Carlo	Jody Scheckter	Wolf WR1-Cosworth
Belgian GP	Zolder	Gunnar Nilsson	Lotus 78-Cosworth
Swedish GP	Anderstorp	Jacques Laffite	Ligier JS7-Matra
French GP	Dijon-Prenois	Mario Andretti	Lotus 78-Cosworth
British GP	Silverstone	James Hunt	McLaren M26-Cosworth
German GP	Hockenheim	Niki Lauda	Ferrari 312T2
Austrian GP	Österreichring	Alan Jones	Shadow DN8A-Cosworth
Dutch GP	Zandvoort	Niki Lauda	Ferrari 312T2
Italian GP	Monza	Mario Andretti	Lotus 78-Cosworth
US (East) GP	Watkins Glen	James Hunt	McLaren M26-Cosworth
Canadian GP	Mosport	Jody Scheckter	Wolf WR1-Cosworth
Japanese GP	Mount Fuji	James Hunt	McLaren M26-Cosworth

1978 Champion: Mario Andretti

Argentinian GP	Buenos Aires	Mario Andretti	Lotus 78-Cosworth
Brazilian GP	Jacarepaguá	Carlos Reutemann	Ferrari 312T2
South African GP	Kyalami	Ronnie Peterson	Lotus 78-Cosworth
US (West) GP	Long Beach	Carlos Reutemann	Ferrari 312T3
Monaco GP	Monte Carlo	Patrick Depailler	Tyrrell 008-Cosworth
Belgian GP	Zolder	Mario Andretti	Lotus 79-Cosworth
Spanish GP	Jarama	Mario Andretti	Lotus 79-Cosworth
Swedish GP	Anderstorp	Niki Lauda	Brabham BT46B-Alfa Romeo
French GP	Paul Ricard	Mario Andretti	Lotus 79-Cosworth
British GP	Brands Hatch	Carlos Reutemann	Ferrari 312T3
German GP	Hockenheim	Mario Andretti	Lotus 79-Cosworth
Austrian GP	Österreichring	Ronnie Peterson	Lotus 79-Cosworth
Dutch GP	Zandvoort	Mario Andretti	Lotus 79-Cosworth
Italian GP	Monza	Niki Lauda	Brabham BT46-Alfa Romeo
US (East) GP	Watkins Glen	Carlos Reutemann	Ferrari 312T3
Canadian GP	Montreal	Gilles Villeneuve	Ferrari 312T3

1979 Champion: Jody Scheckter

Argentinian GP	Buenos Aires	Jacques Laffite	Ligier JS11-Cosworth
Brazilian GP	Interlagos	Jacques Laffite	Ligier JS11-Cosworth
South African GP	Kyalami	Gilles Villeneuve	Ferrari 312T4
US (West) GP	Long Beach	Gilles Villeneuve	Ferrari 312T4
Spanish GP	Jarama	Patrick Depailler	Ligier JS11-Cosworth
Belgian GP	Zolder	Jody Scheckter	Ferrari 312T4
Monaco GP	Monte Carlo	Jody Scheckter	Ferrari 312T4
French GP	Dijon-Prenois	Jean-Pierre Jabouille	Renault RS10
British GP	Silverstone	Clay Regazzoni	Williams FW07-Cosworth
German GP	Hockenheim	Alan Jones	Williams FW07-Cosworth
Austrian GP	Österreichring	Alan Jones	Williams FW07-Cosworth
Dutch GP	Zandvoort	Alan Jones	Williams FW07-Cosworth
Italian GP	Monza	Jody Scheckter	Ferrari 312T4
Canadian GP	Montreal	Alan Jones	Williams FW07-Cosworth
US GP	Watkins Glen	Gilles Villeneuve	Ferrari 312T4

1980 Champion: Alan Jones

Argentinian GP	Buenos Aires	Alan Jones	Williams FW07-Cosworth
Brazilian GP	Interlagos	René Arnoux	Renault RE21
South African GP	Kyalami	René Arnoux	Renault RE21
US (West) GP	Long Beach	Nelson Piquet	Brabham BT49-Cosworth
Belgian GP	Zolder	Didier Pironi	Ligier JS11/15-Cosworth
Monaco GP	Monte Carlo	Carlos Reutemann	Williams FW07B-Cosworth
French GP	Paul Ricard	Alan Jones	Williams FW07B-Cosworth
British GP	Brands Hatch	Alan Jones	Williams FW07B-Cosworth
German GP	Hockenheim	Jacques Laffite	Ligier JS11/15-Cosworth
Austrian GP	Österreichring	Jean-Pierre Jabouille	Renault RE23
Dutch GP	Zandvoort	Nelson Piquet	Brabham BT49-Cosworth
Italian GP	Imola	Nelson Piquet	Brabham BT49-Cosworth
Canadian GP	Montreal	Alan Jones	Williams FW07B-Cosworth
US (East) GP	Watkins Glen	Alan Jones	Williams FW07B-Cosworth

1981 Champion: Nelson Piquet

US (West) GP	Long Beach	Alan Jones	Williams FW07C-Cosworth
Brazilian GP	Jacarepaguá	Carlos Reutemann	Williams FW07C-Cosworth
Argentinian GP	Buenos Aires	Nelson Piquet	Brabham BT49C-Cosworth
San Marino GP	Imola	Nelson Piquet	Brabham BT49C-Cosworth
Belgian GP	Zolder	Carlos Reutemann	Williams FW07C-Cosworth
Monaco GP	Monte Carlo	Gilles Villeneuve	Ferrari 126C
Spanish GP	Jarama	Gilles Villeneuve	Ferrari 126C
French GP	Dijon-Prenois	Alain Prost	Renault RE30
British GP	Silverstone	John Watson	McLaren MP4-Cosworth
German GP	Hockenheim	Nelson Piquet	Brabham BT49C-Cosworth
Austrian GP	Österreichring	Jacques Laffite	Ligier JS17-Matra
Dutch GP	Zandvoort	Alain Prost	Renault RE30
Italian GP	Monza	Alain Prost	Renault RE30
Canadian GP	Montreal	Jacques Laffite	Ligier JS17-Matra
US GP	Las Vegas	Alan Jones	Williams FW07C-Cosworth

1982 Champion: Keke Rosberg

South African GP	Kyalami	Alain Prost	Renault RE30B
Brazilian GP	Jacarepaguá	Alain Prost	Renault RE30B
US (West) GP	Long Beach	Niki Lauda	McLaren MP4B-Cosworth
San Marino GP	Imola	Didier Pironi	Ferrari 126C2
Belgian GP	Zolder	John Watson	McLaren MP4B-Cosworth
Monaco GP	Monte Carlo	Riccardo Patrese	Brabham BT49D-Cosworth
US (East) GP	Detroit	John Watson	McLaren MP4B-Cosworth
Canadian GP	Montreal	Nelson Piquet	Brabham BT50-BMW
Dutch GP	Zandvoort	Didier Pironi	Ferrari 126C2
British GP	Brands Hatch	Niki Lauda	McLaren MP4B-Cosworth
French GP	Paul Ricard	René Arnoux	Renault RE30B
German GP	Hockenheim	Patrick Tambay	Ferrari 126C2
Austrian GP	Österreichring	Elio de Angelis	Lotus 91-Cosworth
Swiss GP	Dijon-Prenois	Keke Rosberg	Williams FW08-Cosworth
Italian GP	Monza	René Arnoux	Renault RE30B
US GP	Las Vegas	Michele Alboreto	Tyrrell 011-Cosworth

1983 Champion: Nelson Piquet

Brazilian GP	Jacarepaguá	Nelson Piquet	Brabham BT52-BMW
US (West) GP	Long Beach	John Watson	McLaren MP4/1C-Cosworth
French GP	Paul Ricard	Alain Prost	Renault RE40
San Marino GP	Imola	Patrick Tambay	Ferrari 126C2B
Monaco GP	Monte Carlo	Keke Rosberg	Williams FW08C-Cosworth
Belgian GP	Spa-Francorchamps	Alain Prost	Renault RE40
US (East) GP	Detroit	Michele Alboreto	Tyrrell 011-Cosworth
Canadian GP	Montreal	René Arnoux	Ferrari 126C2B
British GP	Silverstone	Alain Prost	Renault RE40
German GP	Hockenheim	René Arnoux	Ferrari 126C3
Austrian GP	Österreichring	Alain Prost	Renault RE40
Dutch GP	Zandvoort	René Arnoux	Ferrari 126C3
Italian GP	Monza	Nelson Piquet	Brabham BT52B-BMW
European GP	Brands Hatch	Nelson Piquet	Brabham BT52B-BMW
South African GP	Kyalami	Riccardo Patrese	Brabham BT52B-BMW

1984 Champion: Niki Lauda

Brazilian GP	Jacarepaguá	Alain Prost	McLaren MP4/2-TAG
South African GP	Kyalami	Niki Lauda	McLaren MP4/2-TAG
Belgian GP	Zolder	Michele Alboreto	Ferrari 126C4
San Marino GP	Imola	Alain Prost	McLaren MP4/2-TAG
French GP	Dijon-Prenois	Niki Lauda	McLaren MP4/2-TAG
Monaco GP	Monte Carlo	Alain Prost	McLaren MP4/2-TAG
Canadian GP	Montreal	Nelson Piquet	Brabham BT53-BMW
US (East) GP	Detroit	Nelson Piquet	Brabham BT53-BMW
US GP	Dallas	Keke Rosberg	Williams FW09-Honda
British GP	Brands Hatch	Niki Lauda	McLaren MP4/2-TAG
German GP	Hockenheim	Alain Prost	McLaren MP4/2-TAG
Austrian GP	Österreichring	Niki Lauda	McLaren MP4/2-TAG
Dutch GP	Zandvoort	Alain Prost	McLaren MP4/2-TAG
Italian GP	Monza	Niki Lauda	McLaren MP4/2-TAG
European GP	Nürburgring	Alain Prost	McLaren MP4/2-TAG
Portuguese GP	Estoril	Alain Prost	McLaren MP4/2-TAG

1985 Champion: Alain Prost

Brazilian GP	Jacarepaguá	Alain Prost	McLaren MP4/2B-TAG
Portuguese GP	Estoril	Ayrton Senna	Lotus 97T-Renault
San Marino GP	Imola	Elio de Angelis	Lotus 97T-Renault
Monaco GP	Monte Carlo	Alain Prost	McLaren MP4/2B-TAG
Canadian GP	Montreal	Michele Alboreto	Ferrari 156/85
US GP	Detroit	Keke Rosberg	Williams FW10-Honda
French GP	Paul Ricard	Nelson Piquet	Brabham BT54-BMW
British GP	Silverstone	Alain Prost	McLaren MP4/2B-TAG
German GP	Nürburgring	Michele Alboreto	Ferrari 156/85
Austrian GP	Österreichring	Alain Prost	McLaren MP4/2B-TAG
Dutch GP	Zandvoort	Niki Lauda	McLaren MP4/2B-TAG
Italian GP	Monza	Alain Prost	McLaren MP4/2B-TAG
Belgian GP	Spa-Francorchamps	Ayrton Senna	Lotus 97T-Renault
European GP	Brands Hatch	Nigel Mansell	Williams FW10-Honda
South African GP	Kyalami	Nigel Mansell	Williams FW10-Honda
Australian GP	Adelaide	Keke Rosberg	Williams FW10-Honda

1986 Champion: Alain Prost

Brazilian GP	Jacarepaguá	Nelson Piquet	Williams FW11-Honda
Spanish GP	Jerez	Ayrton Senna	Lotus 98T-Renault
San Marino GP	Imola	Alain Prost	McLaren MP4/2C-TAG
Monaco GP	Monte Carlo	Alain Prost	McLaren MP4/2C-TAG
Belgian GP	Spa-Francorchamps	Nigel Mansell	Williams FW11-Honda
Canadian GP	Montreal	Nigel Mansell	Williams FW11-Honda
US GP	Detroit	Ayrton Senna	Lotus 98T-Renault
French GP	Paul Ricard	Nigel Mansell	Williams FW11-Honda
British GP	Brands Hatch	Nigel Mansell	Williams FW11-Honda
German GP	Hockenheim	Nelson Piquet	Williams FW11-Honda
Hungarian GP	Hungaroring	Nelson Piquet	Williams FW11-Honda

Austrian GP	Österreichring	Alain Prost	McLaren MP4/2C-TAG
Italian GP	Monza	Nelson Piquet	Williams FW11-Honda
Portuguese GP	Estoril	Nigel Mansell	Williams FW11-Honda
Mexican GP	Mexico City	Gerhard Berger	Benetton B186-BMW
Australian GP	Adelaide	Alain Prost	McLaren MP4/2C-TAG

1987 Champion: Nelson Piquet

Brazilian GP	Jacarepaguá	Alain Prost	McLaren MP4/3-TAG
San Marino GP	Imola	Nigel Mansell	Williams FW11B-Honda
Belgian GP	Spa-Francorchamps	Alain Prost	McLaren MP4/3-TAG
Monaco GP	Monte Carlo	Ayrton Senna	Lotus 99T-Honda
US GP	Detroit	Ayrton Senna	Lotus 99T-Honda
French GP	Paul Ricard	Nigel Mansell	Williams FW11B-Honda
British GP	Silverstone	Nigel Mansell	Williams FW11B-Honda
German GP	Hockenheim	Nelson Piquet	Williams FW11B-Honda
Hungarian GP	Hungaroring	Nelson Piquet	Williams FW11B-Honda
Austrian GP	Österreichring	Nigel Mansell	Williams FW11B-Honda
Italian GP	Monza	Nelson Piquet	Williams FW11B-Honda
Portuguese GP	Estoril	Alain Prost	McLaren MP4/3-TAG
Spanish GP	Jerez	Nigel Mansell	Williams FW11B-Honda
Mexican GP	Mexico City	Nigel Mansell	Williams FW11B-Honda
Japanese GP	Suzuka	Gerhard Berger	Ferrari F187
Australian GP	Adelaide	Gerhard Berger	Ferrari F187

1988 Champion: Ayrton Senna

Brazilian GP	Jacarepaguá	Alain Prost	McLaren MP4/4-Honda
San Marino GP	Imola	Ayrton Senna	McLaren MP4/4-Honda
Monaco GP	Monte Carlo	Alain Prost	McLaren MP4/4-Honda
Mexican GP	Mexico City	Alain Prost	McLaren MP4/4-Honda
Canadian GP	Montreal	Ayrton Senna	McLaren MP4/4-Honda
US GP	Detroit	Ayrton Senna	McLaren MP4/4-Honda
French GP	Paul Ricard	Alain Prost	McLaren MP4/4-Honda
British GP	Silverstone	Ayrton Senna	McLaren MP4/4-Honda
German GP	Hockenheim	Ayrton Senna	McLaren MP4/4-Honda
Hungarian GP	Hungaroring	Ayrton Senna	McLaren MP4/4-Honda
Belgian GP	Spa-Francorchamps	Ayrton Senna	McLaren MP4/4-Honda
Italian GP	Monza	Gerhard Berger	Ferrari F187/88C
Portuguese GP	Estoril	Alain Prost	McLaren MP4/4-Honda
Spanish GP	Jerez	Alain Prost	McLaren MP4/4-Honda
Japanese GP	Suzuka	Ayrton Senna	McLaren MP4/4-Honda
Australian GP	Adelaide	Alain Prost	McLaren MP4/4-Honda

1989 Champion: Alain Prost

Brazilian GP	Jacarepaguá	Nigel Mansell	Ferrari 640
San Marino GP	Imola	Ayrton Senna	McLaren MP4/5-Honda
Monaco GP	Monte Carlo	Ayrton Senna	McLaren MP4/5-Honda
Mexican GP	Mexico City	Ayrton Senna	McLaren MP4/5-Honda
US GP	Phoenix	Alain Prost	McLaren MP4/5-Honda
Canadian GP	Montreal	Thierry Boutsen	Williams FW12C-Renault
French GP	Paul Ricard	Alain Prost	McLaren MP4/5-Honda
British GP	Silverstone	Alain Prost	McLaren MP4/5-Honda
German GP	Hockenheim	Ayrton Senna	McLaren MP4/5-Honda
Hungarian GP	Hungaroring	Nigel Mansell	Ferrari 640
Belgian GP	Spa-Francorchamps	Ayrton Senna	McLaren MP4/5-Honda
Italian GP	Monza	Alain Prost	McLaren MP4/5-Honda
Portuguese GP	Estoril	Gerhard Berger	Ferrari 640
Spanish GP	Jerez	Ayrton Senna	McLaren MP4/5-Honda
Japanese GP	Suzuka	Alessandro Nannini	Benetton B189-Ford
Australian GP	Adelaide	Thierry Boutsen	Williams FW13-Renault

1990 Champion: Ayrton Senna

US GP	Phoenix	Ayrton Senna	McLaren MP4/5B-Honda
Brazilian GP	Interlagos	Alain Prost	Ferrari 641
San Marino GP	Imola	Riccardo Patrese	Williams FW13B-Renault
Monaco GP	Monte Carlo	Ayrton Senna	McLaren MP4/5B-Honda
Canadian GP	Montreal	Ayrton Senna	McLaren MP4/5B-Honda
Mexican GP	Mexico City	Alain Prost	Ferrari 641/2
French GP	Paul Ricard	Alain Prost	Ferrari 641/2
British GP	Silverstone	Alain Prost	Ferrari 641/2
German GP	Hockenheim	Ayrton Senna	McLaren MP4/5B-Honda
Hungarian GP	Hungaroring	Thierry Boutsen	Williams FW13B-Renault
Belgian GP	Spa-Francorchamps	Ayrton Senna	McLaren MP4/5B-Honda
Italian GP	Monza	Ayrton Senna	McLaren MP4/5B-Honda
Portuguese GP	Estoril	Nigel Mansell	Ferrari 641/2
Spanish GP	Jerez	Alain Prost	Ferrari 641/2
Japanese GP	Suzuka	Nelson Piquet	Benetton B190-Ford
Australian GP	Adelaide	Nelson Piquet	Benetton B190-Ford

1991 Champion: Ayrton Senna

US GP	Phoenix	Ayrton Senna	McLaren MP4/6-Honda
Brazilian GP	Interlagos	Ayrton Senna	McLaren MP4/6-Honda
San Marino GP	Imola	Ayrton Senna	McLaren MP4/6-Honda
Monaco GP	Monte Carlo	Ayrton Senna	McLaren MP4/6-Honda
Canadian GP	Montreal	Nelson Piquet	Benetton B191-Ford
Mexican GP	Mexico City	Riccardo Patrese	Williams FW14-Renault
French GP	Magny-Cours	Nigel Mansell	Williams FW14-Renault
British GP	Silverstone	Nigel Mansell	Williams FW14-Renault
German GP	Hockenheim	Nigel Mansell	Williams FW14-Renault
Hungarian GP	Hungaroring	Ayrton Senna	McLaren MP4/6-Honda
Belgian GP	Spa-Francorchamps	Ayrton Senna	McLaren MP4/6-Honda
Italian GP	Monza	Nigel Mansell	Williams FW14-Renault
Portuguese GP	Estoril	Riccardo Patrese	Williams FW14-Renault
Spanish GP	Catalunya	Nigel Mansell	Williams FW14-Renault
Japanese GP	Suzuka	Gerhard Berger	McLaren MP4/6-Honda
Australian GP	Adelaide	Ayrton Senna	McLaren MP4/6-Honda

1992 Champion: Nigel Mansell

South African GP	Kyalami	Nigel Mansell	Williams FW14B-Renault
Mexican GP	Mexico City	Nigel Mansell	Williams FW14B-Renault
Brazilian GP	Interlagos	Nigel Mansell	Williams FW14B-Renault
Spanish GP	Catalunya	Nigel Mansell	Williams FW14B-Renault
San Marino GP	Imola	Nigel Mansell	Williams FW14B-Renault
Monaco GP	Monte Carlo	Ayrton Senna	McLaren MP4/7A-Honda
Canadian GP	Montreal	Gerhard Berger	McLaren MP4/7A-Honda
French GP	Magny-Cours	Nigel Mansell	Williams FW14B-Renault
British GP	Silverstone	Nigel Mansell	Williams FW14B-Renault
German GP	Hockenheim	Nigel Mansell	Williams FW14B-Renault
Hungarian GP	Hungaroring	Ayrton Senna	McLaren MP4/7A-Honda
Belgian GP	Spa-Francorchamps	Michael Schumacher	Benetton B192-Ford
Italian GP	Monza	Ayrton Senna	McLaren MP4/7A-Honda
Portuguese GP	Estoril	Nigel Mansell	Williams FW14B-Renault
Japanese GP	Suzuka	Riccardo Patrese	Williams FW14B-Renault
Australian GP	Adelaide	Gerhard Berger	McLaren MP4/7A-Honda

1993 Champion: Alain Prost

South African GP	Kyalami	Alain Prost	Williams FW15C-Renault
Brazilian GP	Interlagos	Ayrton Senna	McLaren MP4/8-Ford
European GP	Donington Park	Ayrton Senna	McLaren MP4/8-Ford
San Marino GP	Imola	Alain Prost	Williams FW15C-Renault
Spanish GP	Catalunya	Alain Prost	Williams FW15C-Renault
Monaco GP	Monte Carlo	Ayrton Senna	McLaren MP4/8-Ford
Canadian GP	Montreal	Alain Prost	Williams FW15C-Renault
French GP	Magny-Cours	Alain Prost	Williams FW15C-Renault
British GP	Silverstone	Alain Prost	Williams FW15C-Renault
German GP	Hockenheim	Alain Prost	Williams FW15C-Renault
Hungarian GP	Hungaroring	Damon Hill	Williams FW15C-Renault
Belgian GP	Spa-Francorchamps	Damon Hill	Williams FW15C-Renault
Italian GP	Monza	Damon Hill	Williams FW15C-Renault
Portuguese GP	Estoril	Michael Schumacher	Benetton B193B-Ford
Japanese GP	Suzuka	Ayrton Senna	McLaren MP4/8-Ford
Australian GP	Adelaide	Ayrton Senna	McLaren MP4/8-Ford

1994 Champion: Michael Schumacher

Brazilian GP	Interlagos	Michael Schumacher	Benetton B194-Ford
Pacific GP	Tanaka International	Michael Schumacher	Benetton B194-Ford
San Marino GP	Imola	Michael Schumacher	Benetton B194-Ford
Monaco GP	Monte Carlo	Michael Schumacher	Benetton B194-Ford
Spanish GP	Catalunya	Damon Hill	Williams FW16-Renault
Canadian GP	Montreal	Michael Schumacher	Benetton B194-Ford
French GP	Magny-Cours	Michael Schumacher	Benetton B194-Ford
British GP	Silverstone	Damon Hill	Williams FW16-Renault
German GP	Hockenheim	Gerhard Berger	Ferrari 412T1B
Hungarian GP	Hungaroring	Michael Schumacher	Benetton B194-Ford
Belgian GP	Spa-Francorchamps	Damon Hill	Williams FW16B-Renault
Italian GP	Monza	Damon Hill	Williams FW16B-Renault
Portuguese GP	Estoril	Damon Hill	Williams FW16B-Renault
European GP	Jerez	Michael Schumacher	Benetton B194-Ford
Japanese GP	Suzuka	Damon Hill	Williams FW16B-Renault
Australian GP	Adelaide	Nigel Mansell	Williams FW16B-Renault

1995 Results at time of going to press

Brazilian GP	Interlagos	Michael Schumacher	Benetton B195-Renault
Argentinian GP	Buenos Aires	Damon Hill	Williams FW17-Renault
San Marino GP	Imola	Damon Hill	Williams FW17-Renault

Name	Wins	Seconds	Thirds	Pole positions	Fastest laps	Starts	Points
Michele Alboreto (I) b.1956	5	9	9	2	5	194	186¹/₂
Mario Andretti (USA) b.1940	12	2	5	18	10	128	180
Elio de Angelis (I)1958-1986	2	2	5	3	–	108	122
René Arnoux (F) b.1948	7	9	7	18	12	149	181
Alberto Ascari (I) 1918-1955	13	4	–	14	11	32	139
Giancarlo Baghetti (I) b.1934	1	–	–	–	1	21	14
Lorenzo Bandini (I) 1935-1967	1	2	5	1	2	42	58
Jean-Pierre Beltoise (F) b.1937	1	3	4	–	4	85	77
Gerhard Berger (A) b.1959	9	15	16	10	17	166	315
Joakim Bonnier (S) 1930-1972	1	–	–	1	–	102	39
Thierry Boutsen (B) b.1957	3	2	10	1	1	163	132
Jack Brabham (AUS) b.1926	14	10	8	13	10	126	261
Vittorio Brambilla (I) b. 1937	1	–	–	1	2	74	15¹/₂
Tony Brooks (GB) b.1932	6	2	2	3	3	38	75
François Cevert (F) 1944-1973	1	10	2	–	2	46	89
Jim Clark (GB) 1936-1968	25	1	6	33	27	72	274
Peter Collins (GB) 1931-1958	3	3	3	1	–	32	47
Patrick Depailler (F) 1944-1980	2	10	7	1	4	93	141
Juan Manuel Fangio (RA) b.1911	24	11	1	28	23	51	277¹/₂
Giuseppe Farina (I) 1906-1966	5	9	6	5	6	33	128¹/₃
Emerson Fittipaldi (BR) b.1946	14	13	8	6	6	144	281
Peter Gethin (GB) b.1940	1	–	–	–	–	30	11
Richie Ginther (USA) 1930-1989	1	8	5	–	3	52	107
Froilan Gonzalez (RA) b.1922	1	7	6	3	6	26	77¹/₂
Dan Gurney (USA) b.1931	4	8	7	3	7	86	133
Mike Hawthorn (GB)1929-1959	3	9	6	4	6	45	127¹/₂
Damon Hill (GB) b.1960	11	9	3	5	11	37	180
Graham Hill (GB) 1929-1975	14	15	7	13	10	176	289
Phil Hill (USA) b.1927	3	6	7	6	6	48	98
Denny Hulme (NZ) 1936-1992	8	9	17	1	9	112	248
James Hunt (GB) 1947-1993	10	6	7	14	8	92	179
Jacky Ickx (B) b.1945	8	7	10	13	14	116	181
Innes Ireland (GB) 1930-1993	1	2	1	–	1	50	47
Jean-Pierre Jabouille (F) b.1942	2	–	–	6	–	49	21
Alan Jones (AUS) b.1946	12	7	5	6	13	116	206
Jacques Laffite (F) b.1943	6	9	16	7	7	175	228
Niki Lauda (A) b.1949	25	20	9	24	25	171	420¹/₂
Nigel Mansell (GB) b.1954	31	17	11	32	30	186	482
Jochen Mass (D) b.1946	1	1	6	–	2	105	71
Bruce McLaren (NZ) 1937-1970	4	11	12	–	3	101	198¹/₂
Stirling Moss (GB) b.1929	16	5	2	16	20	66	186¹/₂
Alessandro Nannini (I) b.1959	1	2	6	–	2	77	65
Gunnar Nilsson (S) 1948-1978	1	–	3	–	–	31	31
Carlos Pace (BR) 1944-1977	1	3	2	1	5	72	58
Riccardo Patrese (I) b.1954	6	17	14	8	13	256	281
Ronnie Peterson (S) 1944-1978	10	10	6	14	9	123	206
Nelson Piquet (BR) b.1952	23	20	17	24	23	204	485¹/₂
Didier Pironi (F) 1952-1987	3	3	7	4	6	70	101
Alain Prost (F) b.1955	51	35	20	33	41	199	798¹/₂
Clay Regazzoni (CH) b.1939	5	13	10	5	15	132	212
Carlos Reutemann (RA) b.1939	12	13	20	6	4	146	310
Peter Revson (USA) 1939-1974	2	2	4	1	–	30	61
Jochen Rindt (A) 1942-1970	6	3	4	10	3	60	109
Pedro Rodriguez (MEX) 1940-1971	2	3	2	–	1	55	71
Keke Rosberg (SF) b.1948	5	8	4	5	3	114	159¹/₂
Ludovico Scarfiotti (I) 1933-1968	1	–	–	–	1	10	17
Jody Scheckter (ZA) b.1950	10	14	9	3	6	112	255
Michael Schumacher (D) b.1969	11	10	8	7	16	55	215
Ayrton Senna (BR) 1960-1994	41	23	16	65	19	161	614
Jo Siffert (CH) 1936-1971	2	2	2	2	4	97	68
Jackie Stewart (GB) b.1939	27	11	5	17	15	99	360
John Surtees (GB) b.1934	6	10	8	8	11	111	180
Patrick Tambay (F) b.1949	2	4	5	5	2	114	103
Piero Taruffi (I) b.1906	1	3	1	–	1	18	41
Maurice Trintignant (F) b.1917	2	3	5	–	1	82	72¹/₃
Wolfgang von Trips (D) 1928-1961	2	2	2	1	–	27	56
Gilles Villeneuve (CDN) 1952-1982	6	5	2	2	7	67	107
John Watson (GB) b.1946	5	6	9	2	5	152	169

Statistics up to and including 1995 San Marino Grand Prix.